Teaching Kids to Love Learning, Not Just Endure It

Michael Connolly

Rowman & Littlefield Education

A division of
ROWMAN & LITTLEFIELD PUBLISHERS, INC.
Lanham • New York • Toronto • Plymouth, UK

Published by Rowman & Littlefield Education
A division of Rowman & Littlefield Publishers, Inc.
A wholly owned subsidiary of
The Rowman & Littlefield Publishing Group, Inc.
4501 Forbes Boulevard, Suite 200, Lanham, Maryland 20706
http://www.rowmaneducation.com

Estover Road, Plymouth PL6 7PY, United Kingdom

British Library Cataloguing in Publication Information Available

Library of Congress Cataloging-in-Publication Data
Connolly, Michael.
  Teaching kids to love learning, not just endure it / Michael Connolly.
    p. cm.
  Includes bibliographical references.
  ISBN 978-1-60709-957-4 (cloth : alk. paper) — ISBN 978-1-60709-958-1
(pbk. : alk. paper) — ISBN 978-1-60709-959-8 (ebook)
  1. Motivation in education. I. Title.
  LB1065.C64 2011
  370.15'4—dc22   2011011774

∞™ The paper used in this publication meets the minimum requirements
of American National Standard for Information Sciences—Permanence of
Paper for Printed Library Materials, ANSI/NISO Z39.48-1992.

Printed in the United States of America

This book is dedicated to the many educators I have had the privilege of
working with, who understand and honor the importance of love and passion
in the education of young people.

Contents

Acknowledgments

I want to thank the many educators with whom I have worked over the years, who have demonstrated a genuine love for students and a passion for what they teach them. A few of those teachers are mentioned by name in this book. I am grateful to teachers Sandra Hahn, Reno Taini, and Karen Rayle and student Yeon Duk Woo for giving me permission to use their names.

I am grateful also to those many teachers with whom I have worked whose names are not mentioned in the pages that follow but whose heartfelt affection for those they teach and what they teach has inspired this book and its title.

A few of the chapters in this book were originally published as articles in educational journals. I wish to thank the editors of those journals for allowing me to revise those articles and include them in this book. My thanks to Phyllis Konikow, of the National Association of Secondary School Principals, for permission to revise and reuse "Why Education Needs the Arts," which I originally wrote with teacher colleague, Sophie Mason. The original article was published in *Principal Leadership*, November 2009, Vol. 10, No. 3, ©2009 National Association of Secondary School Principals. For more information on NASSP products and services to promote excellence in middle level and high school leadership, visit www.principals.org.

Thanks to Bob Spear, executive director of the New England Association of Middle Schools, for permission to reuse "Making Education Relevant: A Micro-Society Approach," published in the *Journal of the New England League of Middle Schools* (Spring 1994).

My gratitude to David Willows, former editor of the *Journal of Innovative Teaching*, for permission to reuse "Discovering the Wonders of Science," originally published in April 2005.

Thanks to Debra Brydon for permission to revise and reuse the article, "The Parent Walkabout," which originally appeared in the Australian journal *Leadership in Focus* (Winter 2009).

I deeply appreciate the efforts of Charlene Pollano, Paul Moreau, Santha Kumar, and Duncan McCutchan, four people who agreed to read the original manuscript of this book and who offered suggestions for making it better.

This book would never have been finished without the love, support, and frequent critical reading of my wife, Brie Goolbis. Thank you, Brie.

Finally, I want to express my sincere gratitude to my editors at Rowman & Littlefield Education, who have patiently worked with me to bring this book to press. Thank you, Kristina Mann, acquisitions editor, and Tom Koerner, vice president and editorial director, for your patience, encouragement, and assistance. I couldn't have done it without you.

Introduction

The students are restless as I enter the gymnasium, accompanied by an entourage of school board members, the head of school, and student council members. The faculty lean against the back wall with arms folded and a "tell me something I haven't heard before" expression on their faces.

I'm determined to do just that. What I, their new principal, have to say will shock them—students and faculty alike. Not because the words themselves are scandalous or the idea they express outrageous, but because few teachers or administrators ever talk to students about or discuss among themselves what I am about to reveal. And that is our shame.

So, as I wait to be introduced by the head of school, I go over again in my mind the words I will say to the students. *I want to share with you one of the best-kept secrets of school. [Pause] We, your teachers, love you. Yes, love you. No, love isn't too strong a word to describe what we feel for you.*

It is a message I've delivered at times in other schools. It always has the same effect. It leaves the audience stunned. Yet the message never fails to bring expressions of appreciation from students, teachers, and parents after an assembly has ended.

Why then is it so difficult for us to acknowledge this love and speak about it more openly in schools and in classrooms?

Perhaps it is because we have been encouraged to view teacher/student interaction as a business transaction. Perhaps, too, it is because we talk so often about academic rigor and high standards and high-stakes assessments that we have buried (not yet killed, but buried) the heart of teaching and learning. Education should not be viewed as a business transaction, although some would like to see it that way. Teaching and learning are as much affairs of the heart as they are of the mind—and that is something we must never forget.

Roland Barth described the essence of that love relationship from the teacher's perspective in *Learning by Heart*. "Most of us—teachers, principals and other school people—signed up for this profession because we care deeply about our important place in the lives of students. To put it simply: in addition to a brain we have a heart—and we want to put it to use in promoting young people's learning" (2001, p. xxv).

To discover the essence of the love relationship from the pupil's perspective, I spent time analyzing comments (spoken and written) by people, young and older, about what encouraged their learning and what discouraged it.

I examined the remarks of poets, artists, musicians, mathematicians, scientists, political and business leaders, professional athletes, and coaches to uncover what motivates them to learn throughout their lives.

I asked students what "turns them on" and "what turns them off" when they are presented with a new learning opportunity. I reviewed the history of my own learning and asked myself those same questions. You will find respondents' answers and mine in the pages of this book.

Regrettably, many policymakers who express interest in the education of young people haven't taken time to reflect upon their own learning experiences, good or bad, to determine what kinds of actions, their own and those of others, encourage them to continue to pursue the challenge of new learning and which ones reduce or even destroy their motivation to continue.

In neglecting to pay attention to what motivates our own learning, we often miss the things that help us understand what motivates others to learn. Not all the answers to important questions about inspiring love of learning can be found at workshops or in books. Sometimes we must search within for the answers.

What I discovered in my search for answers to how we should educate children if we want them to love learning rather than endure it is not surprising. But it is too easily overshadowed by concerns about curriculum, teaching strategies, test preparation, adequate yearly progress, and accountability.

I discovered, first by looking within and then by analyzing the stories of others, that a student's first romance with a subject is most often orchestrated by an inspired matchmaker—a teacher, a parent, or a mentor who cares deeply about that student, as in "I, your teacher, love you." A teacher or parent or mentor who believes that what she will be teaching a student has the power to transform that student's life into something remarkable cannot help but have a powerful, positive influence on that student.

I recognize the influence of a number of teachers in my life. Father DeSales Standerwick, my high school English teacher, taught me to love words and insisted that I and my classmates use vocabulary clearly, precisely, and expressively in everything we wrote. From him, I learned to value Mark Twain's observation, made in a letter he wrote in 1888, that the "difference between the almost right word & the right word is really a large matter—it's the difference between the lightning bug and the lightning."

In my undergraduate years, Dr. William Burto inflamed my passion for English literature—reading it and writing about it. Fr. DeSales and Dr. Burto were two matchmakers who inspired my love of language and influenced my decision to become an English teacher and later a writer. I will always be grateful to them for their gift of love. When these two conditions are present—the teacher's love for students and her passion for her subject—that passion spreads like a benign infection to pupils.

When one or the other is absent, the teacher may have well-designed curriculum and assessments, a variety of research-based teaching techniques, and a clear set of performance expectations for students and still not be able to inspire students to love learning.

Read how a teacher who cared about his students and was passionate about what he was teaching influenced the life of historian Barbara Tuchman, as she relates in her book *Practicing History*:

> It did not matter to [Professor] McIlwain, a renowned scholar and historian, that only four of us were taking his course, or that he had already given it at Harvard and had come over [to Radcliff] to repeat it to us (yes, that was the quaint custom of the time). It did not matter because McIlwain was conducting a passionate love affair with the laws of the Angles and the articles of the Charter, especially, as I remember, Article 39. *Like any person in love, he wanted to let everyone know how beautiful was the object of his affections.* (1981, p. 14; emphasis added)

And what was the effect of this teacher's desire to share the *object of his affections* with students he cared about? It should not surprise anyone who has had the good fortune to have such a teacher.

> And though I cannot remember a word of Article 39, I do remember how his blue eyes blazed as he discussed it and how I sat on the edge of my seat then too, and how, to show my appreciation, I would have given anything to have written a brilliant exam paper. (Tuchman 1981, p. 14)

A final word. Throughout the pages of this book, I will be using the term "teacher" in the broadest sense of that word. Parents are teachers, so are relatives and friends who choose to teach young people important lessons or share their passions with them. So are coaches and counselors. Hey, even the building custodian can be a marvelous teacher, as we learned from the movie *The Karate Kid*.

This book is not just for professional teachers but for anyone who assumes the critical role of trying to educate young people in a way that inspires them to love learning, not just endure it.

CHAPTER SUMMARIES

Introduction

The occasion of my opening address to students and teachers as I assume the position as their new principal serves as an opportunity for me to reveal one of the seldom-discussed secrets about teaching—that it is grounded in love. ("We your teachers love you.") In writing this book, I spent time looking into what inspires individuals (including myself) to continue to learn and what exhausts enthusiasm for learning. I discovered profound truth in Albert Einstein's observation: "Love is a better teacher than duty."

Chapter 1: What Is Love?

In this chapter, I describe what I mean by love and its relation to teaching. I relate an incident in which I taught some of those same students whom I told "We your teachers love you" that the love involves "tough" in addition to "tender" moments.

Chapter 2: Autopsy: An Examination of How to Discourage Love of Learning

A personal experience when I was ten years old demonstrates how easily learning can be discouraged. I argue that we must allow for a certain amount of sloppiness if genuine learning is to occur. The chapter ends on an upbeat note as I enter a classroom thirty-five years later and observe a fifth-grade teacher inviting students to take the very pathway to learning that I was discouraged from taking when I was ten.

Chapter 3: Learning Is an Emotional Experience

This chapter opens with a description of the various emotions a learner may feel when confronted with a challenging new learning experience. It gives reasons why it is important for teachers to build emotional components into their learning activities.

Chapter 4: Defying the Current Teaching Paradigm

The way a teacher structures a learning experience will determine whether or not students bring intellectual muscle to that learning encounter. To design muscular learning experiences, a teacher must be willing to break away from the traditional teaching and learning paradigm found in most classrooms. That is a challenge for any teacher, who must struggle with both internal and external resistance in order to do it. Stories of two teachers who have succeeded in that struggle conclude the chapter.

Chapter 5: Creating a Supportive Learning Environment

Creating a supportive learning environment is critical for success in a classroom. This chapter describes the strategies that three teachers use to establish trust in their classrooms.

Chapter 6: A Remedy for What Ails Education

Too much focus on technique can cause problems for a teacher by overshadowing the most fundamental factor for success in teaching—the love of a teacher for her students and her passion for her subject.

Chapter 7: Another Love: A Teacher's Passion for Her Discipline

The twin towers on which a teacher can elevate her students' love of learning are her love for her students and her passion for a subject. This chapter talks about the latter of those two.

Chapter 8: Discipline: The Gift of Love

When you talk about the importance of love to learning, some people think you are an educational sissy, but a teacher's love should be both tough and tender, as the story of Mrs. Martin and Robert demonstrates. This chapter also reveals how some attempts to discipline can have unexpected consequences.

Chapter 9: Bringing "Awesome" Back into the Classroom

"Awesome!" Years ago this was one of the most overused words in an adolescent's vocabulary. We don't hear it much anymore, particularly in a classroom. How can we bring the experience of "awesome" back into the classroom? Strategies for doing so and for avoiding "boring" are discussed in this chapter.

Chapter 10: Restoring the Joy to Learning

Can we restore joy to learning? This chapter describes four ways to accomplish this.

Chapter 11: When Learning Isn't Fun

What can a teacher do to guide students through those difficult times when learning isn't fun?

Chapter 12: Education Should Nourish the Spirit

Almost all the conversation we hear about education these days is about preparing students for future employment. But is that all there is to a quality education? What are we doing in classrooms to nourish the spirits of young people? This chapter offers some suggestions about what we should be doing.

Chapter 13: When Education Fails to Nourish the Spirit

In his short story "Expelled," John Cheever described an education that focused so steadfastly on getting students into college that it failed to nourish his spirit and, as a result, led to his being expelled from school. The problem Cheever described is still very much with us today. We must develop a broader perspective on what constitutes "an education" if we hope to fully engage our students in it.

Chapter 14: What's So Right about Being Wrong?

"Wrong"—such an unlovely word! Yet there is much to be gained from being wrong, as every successful scientist, inventor, entrepreneur, and artist knows. Being wrong, or only partially right, is seldom honored in schools—and that has to change.

Chapter 15: What's So Right about Being Wrong?—An Example

A teacher's mistake in a classroom and a student's pointing it out should be cause for celebration?

Chapter 16: Learning to Love *Their* Questions

Young children are notorious for asking a multitude of questions. When they get into school, their question-asking prowess seems to disappear. What is happening in classrooms to discourage student questions, and what can we do to encourage more student questions?

Chapter 17: Teaching Students to Value Commitment

The movie *The Karate Kid* demonstrates why it is so critical for teachers to take the time to structure lessons that teach students to value commitment.

Chapter 18: Revising Our Reductionist View of Teaching and Learning

There is a popular notion that teachers are merely technicians and, if we can just give them the right tools and teach them to use them, then improvement in student performance will naturally follow. But there are qualitative differences between technicians and teachers, and this chapter describes why we need teachers, not technicians, in the classroom.

Chapter 19: We Don't Just Love You, We Need You

Adults tend to underestimate the ability of young people to make significant contributions to our society, but an incident during the Gulf War brought students in one school to national attention and demonstrated the remarkable social contributions that young people are capable of making.

Chapter 20: Learning to Love Unlearning

Part of teaching students to love learning will involve teaching them to love unlearning as well. Opening with an experience I had struggling to unlearn some of my driving habits when I moved to Thailand, I discuss things teachers must do to lead students to love learning's companion—unlearning.

Chapter 21: Discovering the Wonder of Science

Carrying forward a theme from previous chapters, this chapter tells how I discovered the "wonder" of science years after I left school. This chapter has some ideas about how we can stimulate students' excitement not just for science but for any subject.

Chapter 22: Are You a Wonder-Filled Teacher?

As a teacher, are you still filled with wonder and curiosity? Do you openly display that wonder and curiosity when you are working with young people? This chapter talks about why you should.

Chapter 23: Education for Living

"Knowledge without wisdom is a load of books on the back of an ass," a Japanese proverb cautions. We need to spend more time educating students for wisdom, and this chapter offers some thoughts on how we might accomplish that task.

Chapter 24: We Must Love Children in the Concrete, Not Just in the Abstract

Ask most Americans if their nation loves its children, and they would be swift to assure you it does. But the evidence indicates that while America may love its children in the abstract, it has mostly failed to love them in the concrete. This chapter discusses why educators must take the lead in showing the nation what it must do if it is to love children as more than simply an abstraction.

Chapter 25: Making Education Relevant: A Micro-Society Approach

The Micro-Society school is an inspiring approach to educating students that prepares them for full participation in a democratic society. This chapter details how a group of teachers created their own Micro-Society school and what their students gained from that experience.

Chapter 26: Why We Need the Arts in Education

Driven by the clarion calls for more emphasis on math and science in our schools, we may be neglecting subjects that renowned scientist Charles Darwin warned were critical for human happiness, the advancement of moral character, and the development of intellect—the arts.

Chapter 27: Celebrate What's Right with Teaching and Learning

Former Speaker of the House Sam Rayburn used to remind freshman congressional members, "Any jackass can kick down a barn, but it takes a carpenter to build one." It's good advice. Educators need to find ways to celebrate their successes and the successes of their students as a way of sustaining school morale and countering the negativity of others.

Chapter 28: The Walkabout

An easy-to-organize way to make citizens more knowledgeable about what is happening in schools and to get them more involved in and supportive of education.

Chapter 29: Never Lose Sight of the Higher Purpose of an Education

There is a higher purpose for an education than what we read about and hear discussed these days. This chapter identifies that higher purpose and discusses why teachers must never lose sight of it even when others do.

Chapter 30: I Wonder

Having stressed the importance of wonder throughout this book, I share some of the things relating to schooling that I wonder about and encourage readers to do the same.

CHAPTER 1

What Is Love?

"What is love?" a popular song of the 1950s asked. "Five feet of heaven in a ponytail," it responded. The answer seems a bit silly, doesn't it? Still, it's no sillier than many of the contemporary notions that we have about love, so let me define what I mean by love when I speak about it in these pages.

What did I mean when I told the students at that assembly, "We, your teachers, love you"?

I had to trust that no one thought I was referring to sexual attraction. If they did, I'd be out of a job before I even left the stage. Nonetheless, there may have been people in the audience, young and older, who felt that what I meant by "love" was simply the warm and fuzzy feelings of affection that we teachers often have toward at least some of our students.

What I meant by love is something deeper, more rooted than that. As those same students, teachers, and parents would learn later, it included the idea of tough as well as tender love. The definition of the word "love," as I used it then and as I use it here in these pages, is best captured by the idea of doing what you believe is best for someone you care about.

Even the idea of treating others as you would want them to treat you doesn't quite capture what I mean. Too often, the way we'd like to be treated is to have others pamper us, not just treat us respectfully. For many, the idea of love doesn't include attempting to teach the value of discipline or hard work.

An immature view of love is not only unhelpful but also often harmful to those we profess to love. If you have ever watched coddled children attempt to "grow up" or seen adults excusing bad behavior, you know how terrible the effects of such counterfeit love can be.

There is a time for everything, we read in Ecclesiastes: "a time to embrace" (with loving affirmation) and "a time to refrain" (with tough but tender-hearted love) (Ecc. 3:5). Mature love, the kind I was speaking of to that school assembly, knows the proper time for each.

I was in the head of school's office a few months after the assembly when his secretary came in to report that the seniors had walked out of their classes announcing they were on strike (those same seniors who had been in the assembly I had addressed with the words "We, your teachers, love you"). They were sitting on the front lawn refusing to return to classes, demanding a meeting with me, she said.

Before I even reached the strike site, I knew what we'd be talking about.

I'd refused their request to have the song "Closing Time" for their graduation recessional. The song describes the activities at closing time at a bar. I'd nixed it as inappropriate for a graduation. The seniors were furious. Who was I to tell them what song they could or couldn't have for *their* graduation? And besides, hadn't I given them the opportunity to choose their own exit song?

After an hour's discussion about why a graduation wasn't *solely* about them or for them, even though it was a celebration of them and of their accomplishments, I told the seniors that we could continue our discussion, if they wished, on the following day during their recess, but now classes were in session and I expected them to return to theirs.

They balked and refused to move. I told them they had ten minutes to return to class before I started calling them into my office one by one to telephone their parents and have their parents come and take them home. It took seven phone calls before the class sent in representatives to say they'd agree to return to class if we could talk the next day during recess.

When we met the following day, I continued the discussion of why graduation was not only for seniors but also for their parents, relatives, friends, and the school staff, and why a drinking song was inappropriate for such an occasion. Reluctantly they came to accept this.

"There is one more thing," I told them as the meeting was about to break up. "In this school, we do not cut classes; classes are our reason for being in school. Each of you has a choice to make between two options. Either you can attend four half-hour recess sessions with me to make up for the classes you've missed, or I can schedule a conference with your parents. If you prefer not to take the first option, I will explain to your parents why you will be assigned detentions and get a zero for the classes you've missed. Each student can make his or her own choice."

Fury again.

But the next day every senior reported to the makeup class, and everyone came to the three classes after that.

We spent our time reading about and discussing discipline and why it was not something to be avoided but something to be sought after. We talked about why athletes, performers, and soldiers worked hard to develop discipline and what it did for them once they'd developed it.

On the last day, I showed a film clip from *The Karate Kid*. Remember those scenes in which Mr. Miyagi has Daniel polish a parking lot full of cars, sand his deck, paint his fence, and finally paint his house? "No, not that way, like this. Yes, I know it's easier that way, but do it this way."

Remember Daniel's rage when he feels Miyagi is exploiting him? Remember the look of surprise on his face when Miyagi demonstrates for him what all those seemingly mundane menial tasks have taught him? That's where my film clip ended—with that shocked "aha" expression on Daniel's face.

After the final class, several seniors thanked me for taking time to explain what I was requiring of them and why.

However, the best expressions of appreciation came later that year—at graduation. Numbers of seniors and parents thanked me and our faculty for a great graduation, the best ever. By then, I didn't need those expressions of appreciation; they were merely icing on an already beautiful cake. I had my reward. I was so proud of those seniors and how they had conducted themselves throughout the rest of that year, proud of the character and leadership they had shown. What more did I need?

To this day, many years later, I still love that class, every one of them. And who knows, maybe some of them may even love me.

CHAPTER 2

Autopsy: An Examination of How to Discourage Love of Learning

When I was ten years old, I loved to take things apart. I'd dissect them with the excitement of a newly graduated medical student. Old clocks, radios, record players, broken lamps, vacuum cleaners—whatever came my way was a candidate for open-heart surgery. In a matter of minutes, I'd cut into the incapacitated mechanical marvel with precise stabs of my screwdriver and, with a pair of needle-nose pliers, layer by layer, expose the filigree of blue and yellow, red and green veins that made it move or tick.

There was a problem, however. I was a surgeon who seldom sewed up his patients. More often than not, I left them open cadavers on my father's workbench.

This was not so much a problem for me. I knew that I'd return one day to put them back together again, impelled by the same desire that had led me to lay them open in the first place: the desire to discover, to know what made them work. My father, however, viewed my crude surgeries as a blatant example of juvenile sloppiness. He banished me from his workshop.

So at the age of ten, I stopped working with tools and appliances and retreated far away from them, turning my attention to other things. It was an unfortunate choice! To this day, I remain intimidated by things mechanical. I am a klutz when it comes to repairing anything. I must depend on others to fix things for me. No matter how competent I may be in other areas, I rue the lack of competence in this one.

I wish that at age ten I had had the courage to withstand my father's censure. But I did not. More than that, I wish my father had had the patience to stand beside me and watch me take apart the things that were a part of his well-ordered adult world. I wish he had asked me what I was doing and what I was seeing and what I was learning—even when and how I planned to put the things back together again. That would have been a wonderful learning experience—for me and for him. But he did not.

Disapproval is a far less effective teaching tool than affirmation and redirection. Most of us, young or mature, respond more favorably to support than criticism. It isn't because we're thin skinned, either. It is because of the simple fact that affirmation, even when it is accompanied by redirection, encourages us to go forward, while criticism seldom does.

And another thing: learning turns out to be a far messier business than our carefully sequenced, well-ordered plans for making it happen lead us to believe. Learners need to tear things apart, to study them and to gaze in wonder at their innards. That, adults must accept, is an essential part of the seekers' search for knowledge, his attempt to satisfy his thirst for understanding.

It's difficult to accept (I understand this far better now that I am an adult), but what young learners must do as they struggle to understand what we, their elders, have so carefully constructed is to disassemble those constructions in order to appreciate them.

The uncomfortable experience of seeing parts of our well-ordered adult world reduced to shambles and exposed by some young and clumsy surgeon must be endured—even encouraged—as an essential part of how learners learn and how knowledge is advanced. To disassemble something doesn't necessarily mean to destroy it, nor does it always signify an attempt to demean it.

When I was performing my crude autopsies as a ten-year-old, it was not with the intent of destroying my father's world, or dishonoring it. Quite the contrary—I was intent on understanding it with the hope of one day contributing to it.

Thirty-five years after I was banished from my father's workbench, I walked into a classroom to observe a fifth-grade teacher for the first time. As I sat down, I noticed a little area in the back right-hand corner of the room. It had a table with a couple of chairs. On the table were a tool box and an old record player. Above the table on the wall was a very large oak tag poster. It read, "Take-Apart Corner: When you have finished your other work, you are invited to come to this corner and take apart whatever is here and to discover what once made it work."

CHAPTER 3

Learning Is an Emotional Experience

Learning is an emotional, not just an intellectual, experience. The emotions provoked by it vary as in any other life experience. Learners can experience anxiety and fear, and often do, when confronted with a new learning challenge. (Who among us does not experience some anxiety when faced with a new challenge?)

Or one may feel excitement and pleasure, as many of the learners quoted in these pages have. One can experience frustration if the experience is challenging enough. Or the learner can feel fulfillment, even elation, when she is able to persevere through that frustration. The learning experience may lead to fatigue if it is a demanding one.

Often a learner experiences all of these emotions. But shouldn't we expect any experience worthy of the name "learning" to be filled with complex emotions and a variety of ups and downs? The one emotion we don't want learners to feel is the one we too often hear students expressing: "This is boring."

Boredom is the enemy of engagement, and engagement is to learning what motion is to physical exercise—you can't have one without the other. An engaged student brings to the learning experience qualities he needs to master it: curiosity, commitment, alertness, steadfastness, and a sense of purpose.

An unengaged student brings something to a learning task as well: an attitude that is likely to defeat any of his efforts to master it—indifference. Indifference makes a student as unresponsive to the learning stimuli as a rock is to CPR. Unless that attitude is reversed, the student benefits from it as much as the rock does from CPR.

We cannot treat learning as merely a cognitive endeavor and continue to plan lessons without taking into account the emotional quotient that is inherent in it—or should be. Those who plan instructional activities must consider the emotional responses they want students to have in these activities and must design emotional components into their lesson plans.

What constitutes an emotional challenge, and how might we guide young people into it and through it? Emotional challenge is the force produced by emotions aroused in an experience that stretches the learner beyond what she believes she can do and pulls her forward to deeper understanding or even redefinition of what she believes she can accomplish.

When I visit Thailand, as I often do, I work with a team of outdoor adventure instructors. One of the things we do with groups who come to our program is to give them tasks such as getting a group over a fifteen-foot wall with no equipment other than what they have on their bodies. We call this "getting them out of their comfort zone."

That's what an emotional challenge in any learning experience should be designed to do—get people out of their comfort zone so they have to stretch and grow intellectually and emotionally.

Take, for instance, the scene from *Dead Poets Society* where teacher John Keating first meets his students. Notice how he gets them immediately out of their comfort zone. Remember that scene?

The students are comfortably ensconced in their desks, encased in their attitude of ennui, waiting for their teacher to assume his traditional role in front of the class—talking at them. Instead, Keating peeks into the classroom from the hallway and says, "Psst. Well, come on." Then he disappears while the class sits dumbfounded, looking indecisively at one another. No one dares to move until Keating again appears in the doorway and signals them to come on out into the corridor.

Once they arrive there, he positions the class in front of the pictures of former graduates who are now long dead and has one of the current class read Robert Herrick's poem "To the Virgins, to Make Much of Time":

> Gather ye rosebuds while ye may,
> Old Time is still a-flying;
> And this same flower that smiles today
> Tomorrow will be dying.

He instructs his students to lean in closely and listen to what the voices of those dead students are telling them. As they do, he whispers into their circle, "Carpe diem, seize the day, boys."

To say that these boys are now out of their comfort zone with this, their first learning encounter with a new English teacher, is an understatement, but Keating uses this and other emotionally charged learning activities to teach his students a valuable lesson they will not forget. They must seize the moment and work now to make their lives extraordinary.

Emotionally challenging learning experiences force students to examine, explore, and experiment rather than to merely search for and call up "pat answers" from books or lectures. In fact, such lessons often begin by challenging the pat answers. Later in the same movie, Keating has his students tear out the pages in the introduction of their literature book—pages that try to reduce the evaluation of poetry to a formula.

Creative teachers know the importance of structuring learning experiences that generate an emotional response. They know that emotion enhances learning, because we learn not just with our minds but with our bodies as well.

Once these teachers have created an emotionally challenging learning task, they get out of the way and assume the role of a mentor and guide, letting the students struggle with the new task. Each student, they know, must be taught to grapple with and overcome the emotional as well as the cognitive demands of the new learning experience if genuine learning is to take place.

An experienced coach will tell you that you can explain game situations to players and practice and drill them in these situations over and over again, but it is during a real game, when they have to cope with multiple choices and master their own emotions, that players demonstrate whether or not they have learned what they need to do in order to play the game well.

It is only by wrestling with the emotional and cognitive demands of a learning experience that a student can find his own way to mastery, and once he has achieved mastery, he discovers that he can love learning.

Not everyone can take a class to an adventure training course, nor is everyone creative in the same ways as John Keating, but there are multiple ways for creative teachers to design emotional components into their learning activities. Parker Palmer, in *The Courage to Teach*, described how his history of social thought professor introduced cognitive tension into his classes.

> He would make a strong Marxist statement, and we would transcribe it in our notebooks as if it were holy writ. Then a puzzled look would pass over his face. He would pause, step to one side, turn and look back at the space he had just exited—and argue with his own statement from an Hegelian point of view! (1998, p. 136)

Palmer wrote that this was not some kind of artificial teaching device his professor was using but "a genuine expression of the intellectual drama [aka tension] that continually occupied this teacher's mind and heart" (p. 136).

Often we overlook or consciously avoid opportunities to build cognitive tension into our students' learning experiences.

One year in an international school in which I worked, a Christian minister wrote a letter to one of our science teachers asking for an opportunity to challenge a curriculum unit on evolution. The minister wanted to be allowed to come in and present his views on creationism.

The teacher was annoyed and intimidated by the minister's proposal and demanded our head of school and I refuse his request. He argued that evolution had already been established as a scientific fact and creationism had long ago been discredited.

I wish we had not agreed to the teacher's request but had convinced him that there was much to be gained by allowing the minister to present his points of view to the class without proselytizing. Students would have benefited from hearing the different viewpoints and from weighing their own intellectual and emotional responses to those points of view.

Teachers who care deeply about their students and want them to love learning generate emotional engagement in a classroom by designing emotional components and cognitive tension into their students' learning experiences. They know that strong emotion is not an enemy of learning but one of its guardian angels.

CHAPTER 4

Love Demands Defying the Current Teaching Paradigm

Anyone who has ever worked in a school or has on occasion been a visitor to classrooms has observed students confronting the challenge of learning in various ways. Some students come to the task with the wonder of a child studying the flight of a butterfly for the first time—wondering, examining, imagining. Others come as if dragged in chains to a pitiless cell. Most come passively, expecting to be acted upon, to "take it all in" rather than to actively participate. They are, at best, interested spectators in the drama of learning.

But learning—the kind that results in mastery—demands participation. It requires energy, enthusiasm, penetrating powers of observation, thought, and imagination. Bringing a flaccid mind to a learning experience is like bringing a ninety-eight-pound body to compete at muscle beach.

The way a teacher structures a learning encounter is what most often determines whether students bring intellectual muscle to that encounter. Those who have had past experiences sitting, observing, and listening to the teacher or "expert" dispense knowledge, explain ideas, or model how to perform tasks come to new learning experiences expecting more of the same.

When this expectation is validated by similar routines in the new learning situation, the students settle into being spectators again, prepared to regurgitate the information that a teacher or a textbook gives them or to mimic a process that the teacher taught them. This is mindless replication rather than learning. Worse still, it gives students a false sense of what learning is.

Teachers who want students to learn rather than mimic and regurgitate structure classroom experiences so that everyone in the classroom is an actively engaged and contributing member. No intellectual sluggards allowed at this intellectual muscle beach.

This is not as easy as it may sound. To do it, a teacher must defy the current paradigm of classroom teaching—teacher as information giver and student as information gatherer—a paradigm that many teachers and students have become too comfortable with.

Some might suggest that the word "defy" is too strong and that it might be better to settle for a gentler term like "disregard." But "disregard" is simply not an energetic enough word to describe what must be done in order to create a classroom in which students must exercise intellectual muscle to succeed. Why is this so?

To begin with, the first battle a teacher faces is with herself. A teacher usually teaches the way she has been taught. There's nothing terribly surprising about that. The way most teachers have been taught is that a teacher knows a subject and has an obligation to tell students what she knows and students are there to get what she knows.

Thus, the teacher's first act of defiance is usually against herself and her own conviction that this is the way to do things in a classroom. Breaking free from this conviction takes time and usually involves considerable discomfort as the teacher struggles to master and use a new paradigm.

The task is made doubly difficult because in addition to struggling against her own predispositions, the teacher is aware that she must defy the expectation of others who have accepted the myth of teacher as knowledge merchant. The numbers of devotees to this myth are legion, and they are powerful. They include lawmakers, influential members of the community, parents, other educators, and many students.

The mandates of educational reforms like No Child Left Behind and Race to the Top, with their emphasis on accountability as measured by high-stakes assessments, make the task even more daunting. No teacher wants to be labeled a failure or wants her students to be labeled as failures.

Nonetheless, as daunting as the challenge may be, a teacher who cares deeply about her students will summon up the courage to accept the challenge because she recognizes that to become effective learners, students must become active players. She structures learning experiences so that they are engaged participants rather than passive spectators. Teachers all over the world have taken on this challenge and succeeded.

Sandra Hahn was a fourth-grade teacher at the American School of The Hague when I met her. A former opera singer, every year Sandra had her fourth graders write and perform an opera, one of her passions. Now, you can be certain that opera is not in any fourth-grade curriculum, but the opera never failed to be a hit with everyone who witnessed it, and, equally important, Sandra was able to articulate what knowledge and skills that were in the school's curriculum her students learned as a result of the opera activity.

When Sandra speaks to people about her teaching, she talks about getting an umbrella over big ideas in the curriculum rather than focusing on factoids. She'll tell you unapologetically, "Something may be in the curriculum, but if I'm not convinced that it is worthwhile for my students to learn, I won't use it."

Sandra is not intimidated by the specter of criticism because, as she says, "I am my own greatest critic; I am constantly asking myself: What am I doing? Why am I doing it, and why this way?" And because she has confronted her own questions, she is able to address the questions from others when they inevitably come.

She tells them that a teacher must engage each child mentally and physically in a learning experience. To get this mental and physical engagement from each child, says Sandra, a teacher needs to be aware of children's needs and strengths and what will engage each of them. She explains that she structures her classroom according to the following principles:

- Children need to think together with the teacher.
- A teacher needs to help students *grapple* with ideas.
- A teacher needs to teach students to question things and search for their own answers to their questions.
- Children need to learn to discuss ideas with each other—and with their teacher.
- Children need to learn to sort things out and organize ideas.
- Children need to learn to bounce ideas off other people.
- Children need to be involved in planning what they are going to learn. "Other teachers make plans for children; I make plans with them," said Sandra.

These principles foster the idea that in Ms. Hahn's class we are all involved learners and we all have an important role to play in this opera of learning; no one is allowed to assume the role of spectator. No flabby minds allowed in this classroom.

Sandra Hahn may have enjoyed being the star performer in her former role, but she knows students need to be the star performers in a classroom.

Karen Rayle began her teaching experience at Saigon South International School as an ESL (English as a second language) teacher, but when a sixth-grade teacher left in the middle of the school year, she took over as a middle school math/science teacher.

If you entered Karen's classroom on a typical day, you would likely see a student at the whiteboard in the front of the classroom explaining his solution to a math problem, or drawing a picture of how he visualizes a science concept, or presenting an idea or project he is working on. You'll have to search for Karen, who is usually among her other students, listening to those in the front of the room present what they have learned or are working on.

Karen most often begins a unit not by outlining what she will be teaching students in the unit or what will be covered by their textbook, but by asking students to write up at least five questions they each have about the unit they are about to study. Most students come up with many more than five questions; some will have as many as fifty.

Together with the class, Karen then proceeds to divide the students' questions into the following three categories: scientists know this (or think they do) and we can find their answer, scientists are investigating this right now, and this is not really a science question (it may, for instance, be a moral or religious question). Often she graphs the number and kinds of questions students construct to determine just how curious the students are about the topic of a particular unit. Many of the students' questions are similar to those scientists ask. Once the questions are recorded, the class proceeds, as scientists do, to find the answers to them.

Teachers who love what they teach and who are determined to inspire their students to love it too know they cannot accomplish that by allowing students to approach learning as a spectator sport. They recognize that to love learning, a student must engage with it. They understand too that for students to become more active players on the fields of learning, their teacher must function more like a coach than a star performer.

That is not the role that many policymakers, with their command-and-control strategies, are encouraging teachers to adopt. That is why it will take an act of courage for teachers to defy the current classroom teaching paradigm, but those who love children and are determined to teach them to love learning will find the courage to do it. In the process, they will teach students, and perhaps even a few policymakers, what Einstein discovered—"Love is a better teacher than duty."

CHAPTER 5

Creating a Supportive Learning Environment

The best teachers understand something that is little appreciated by less-skilled teachers and by many outside of education who seek to impose change initiatives on schools: Regardless of their age, students learn best in supportive rather than coercive learning environments.

This point has been made convincingly by William Glasser (1990) in *The Quality School* and is reinforced by the American Psychological Association (1995) in its *Learner-Centered Psychological Principles.* Gentle-handed approaches are frequently ignored by our society, where coercion more often than not trumps persuasion as the chosen approach to reaching a goal. What, one might ask, constitutes a supportive environment, and how might those who aspire to create such an environment do it?

To begin, a supportive learning environment is one in which those who teach establish quality personal relationships with their pupils and make it possible for their pupils to develop quality personal relationships with them. Absent quality personal relationships, learning environments seldom thrive.

In a supportive learning environment, it is obvious the teacher cares deeply for his students ("I, your teacher, love you"), and they, in turn, learn to care deeply for him. On the bedrock of this mutual affection, the teacher builds trust with students.

Trust is a vital component of any successful classroom because true learning requires risk taking and because both students and their teacher must willingly take risks that expose their thinking, their flaws, their vulnerabilities, and yes, at times, even their prejudices. Not an easy thing to do.

John Gardner, in his book *Self-Renewal*, pointed out that taking such risks becomes more difficult for most people as they get older:

> By adolescence the willingness of young people to risk failure has diminished greatly. . . . By middle age most of us carry around in our heads a tremendous catalogue of things we have no intention of trying again because we tried them once and failed—or tried them once and did less well than our self-esteem demanded. (1995, p. 14)

In a supportive learning environment, learners, free to express what they are thinking, aren't afraid to take risks. They know that even if their thinking proves flawed or their initial efforts fail, they will not be demeaned by their teacher or peers. They know they will always be treated with respect.

Establishing a supportive learning environment does not simply happen. It requires commitment and sustained effort. It involves setting aside time to get to know your students, allowing them to get to know you, and letting them know you care about them as individuals.

Most of us assume that well-intentioned adults who choose to teach children will take the time to establish a supportive learning environment, but this isn't necessarily the case. Often teachers become so consumed by what they have to teach that they pay little attention to whom they are teaching—those human beings inside those bodies sitting in their desks, the ones seeking not just knowledge and skills but affirmation and support—even the ones who sit sulking in their desks, daring you to love them.

Teachers who establish the kind of trust and respect that are essential for a supportive learning environment verbalize and demonstrate their strong confidence in students' competence and abilities. Their confidence encompasses not only what students can learn but what they can do with their learning. They show this confidence even, and especially, when some of their students don't share it.

Sandra Hahn has fourth graders write and perform their own opera because she knows they are capable of doing it and doing it well—not just some of them, but all of them. How many adults have that kind of faith in fourth graders' ability?

Teachers who create supportive learning environments also recognize that students have knowledge and experiences that must be tapped into and built upon if these students are to continue to learn and grow.

Adults often underestimate what students know and are capable of doing and are sometimes shocked when they see those students display competence in a dramatic performance, or by producing a quality newspaper or literary magazine, by building a house with Habitat for Humanity, or, as fourth graders, by writing and performing their own opera.

Those who create a supportive learning environment don't underestimate their students and what they bring to the classroom. They recognize that "educate" (from the Latin *educare*) means to draw out rather than dump in. They take time to find out what their students already know not just in the subject they are teaching but in other areas as well. They draw upon the knowledge and experience students already have. They involve students in the design of their lessons and in the design of the class's curriculum.

Honoring students' intelligence by involving them in the planning of lessons and curriculum isn't the first step that teachers who establish a supportive learning environment take. The first step is getting to know each student personally and letting students know their teacher as a person, thus building an atmosphere of trust and respect.

Reno Taini works with inner-city students in San Francisco. He has a unique way of initiating this "getting to know you" process. When students enter his classroom at the beginning of a school year, they see a chair draped in red cloth in the center of the room with rows of other chairs encircling it. Over the years, students have taken to dubbing this the "hot seat." Reno simply calls it "center stage" and the "Chair of Respect."

During the first week of school, each member of the class is invited to sit center stage and tell the class about herself. What she likes and doesn't like. What her hopes for the class and the school year might be. The first one onto center stage and into the Chair of Respect is Reno, and he doesn't hold back.

He tells the students about his struggles as a student and as a teacher trying to find his way during his first few years of teaching. He tells them why he loves teaching and working with kids like them. He shares his hopes for the year. After that, it's easier for students to come onto center stage, always in the sacred atmosphere of respect.

The effect that a teacher taking time to establish a personal relationship with a student can have is beautifully documented by Homer Hickman (1998) in his biography, *Rocket Boys*, which was later made into the movie *October Sky*.

It is 1957, and Homer and his three friends have been struggling to build their own rocket after watching the Russian's Sputnik soar across the night sky of their hometown in Coalwood, West Virginia. They are coal miners' sons, and people in the town think the boys are slightly loony for wasting their time trying to build and launch a rocket. But not their teacher, Miss Riley. She doesn't think they are either crazy or incapable of building and launching a rocket. When Homer visits her in the hospital, Miss Riley tells him:

> If you build your own [rocket] you're part of it. I can see that. For me, it's the same with poetry. Sometimes I have to write some of my own—it's poor, I know that—but it allows me to make a connection with the poets I admire. Do you understand?

Homer's reply tells you all you need to know about why a teacher should work to establish a personal relationship with students:

> I think so I told her. No teacher had ever confided in me about anything to do with her personal life the way Miss Riley had just done, almost as if I were her equal. She kept smiling at me, and I felt at that moment like I was the most important person to her in the world. (1998, p. 152)

How's that for developing a communal bond!

Homer, for those of you who may not know it, later went on to work as an aerospace engineer for NASA.

Even when they are pressured by policies like Race to the Top and No Child Left Behind to get on with the business of making students more competitive on international tests, the best teachers recognize there is nothing more important than building a supportive learning environment in their classroom. They know that lacking that supportive learning environment and a strong bond with a teacher who cares about them, many children will inevitably be left behind.

CHAPTER 6

A Remedy for What Ails Education

A perfection of means, and confusion of aims, seems to be our main problem.

Albert Einstein

Technique is important in teaching, as in most other human endeavors: music, art, surgery, construction, baseball. Thoughtful, well-written books on teaching technique make valuable contributions to the teaching profession and to students' learning.

However, excessive focus on teaching technique has created two problems for teachers. The problems are significant because they overshadow a more meaningful truth—one that must be acknowledged in every classroom, indeed in every situation where one person wishes to teach another. I'll get to that truth in just a bit, but first the two problems.

The first problem is easier to deal with than the second. It is this: Those who advocate for a particular teaching practice too often create the impression that their practice is more effective than any others—with all students in all situations. In doing this, they foster the false belief—already prevalent in much of society and sometimes shared by teachers—that there is a silver bullet out there and that if we can get everyone who teaches to grab hold of it, we will overcome all the challenges of educating all students.

Students, like adults, are different and have different experiences, different needs, different learning styles, and different preferences. Thus, there is no such thing as one teaching practice that will serve the needs of all students all the time. The bracing truth is that a successful teacher must learn to use a variety of teaching techniques and strategies.

Bravo! That should be one of the most appealing aspects of teaching. It ensures that teachers, if they want to be effective, must continue to learn and grow and gain new competence just as they expect that students must. Developing good teaching technique alone, though, will never guarantee a teacher success with students.

A second problem—which is likely to be even more challenging to overcome because it aligns with our society's convictions about science—is the belief that there are "scientifically proven" teaching practices. Use them and you can't help but be effective.

We live in an age that believes there are scientific solutions to virtually everything. Many seem to have given up their belief in the power of human judgment in favor of trust in the power of scientific or technological fixes. These individuals and their disciples assure us that teacher-proofed curriculums, computers and computer programs, standardized assessments, and scientifically proven teaching techniques—in other words, anything that doesn't require human judgment—will give us the learning performance we are looking for in schools.

No less a scientist than Nobel Prize–winning physicist Richard Feynman speaking to members of the National Science Teachers Association in 1996 warned us about putting too much faith in those who think this way. Talking about teaching, Feynman said:

> In a field which is so complicated that true science is not able to get anywhere, we have to rely on a kind of old-fashioned wisdom, a kind of definite straightforwardness. I am trying to inspire the teacher at the bottom to have some hope, and some self-confidence in common sense, and natural intelligence. The experts who are leading you may be wrong. (*The Pleasure of Finding Things Out*, p. 187)

So now I turn to that truth about teaching that is overshadowed by endless discussions of teaching techniques—including scientifically proven ones. The prescription that has proven most effective in promoting student learning and love of learning is an older and, as Feynman says, a more "straightforward" one. It was with us before the ascendancy of science. We don't talk much about it anymore, and that is a big part of the problem we have in education.

The love of a teacher for his students and his passion for what he teaches is the strongest medicine that we have to conquer the ennui, which is the greatest obstacle to learning we find in many classrooms.

This is not to disparage technique or any other instruments of instruction. They are valuable additions to a teacher's instructional toolbox, but they are tools. Unless those tools are in the hands of a teacher who cares deeply about students and believes passionately that what he is teaching will enrich student's lives, they will not be as effective as they should be.

A violin is a wonderful instrument and can make beautiful music, but not if it is in the hands of someone who has no love for it and who plays it half-heartedly. The same can be said of any teaching technique used by a teacher who is either indifferent toward his students or lacks passion for what he is teaching—its music will fail to resonate with students.

To the contrary, when a teacher shares his love for a subject with students in the way that Professor McIlwain or Sandra Hahn do, their students come to *love* it too. When that happens, we will have come as close as we ever will to finding a silver bullet for learning.

Most people come into the teaching profession with a love for children and a passion for what they teach. Like Prometheus bearing the gift of fire, they enter the profession longing to set the minds and hearts of their students ablaze. Sadly, discussion of teaching technique has caused many a teacher to lose sight of the power of their love and passion.

Einstein's warning is one that all who seek to teach should take to heart. We talk too much about the methods we use to teach students and so little about what should be the aim of an education—to teach students to love learning.

In neglecting this critical discussion, we create the impression that technique will make the difference in whether or not our students learn, when, in fact, if we can teach them to love learning, they will learn and continue to do so throughout their lives.

The National Basketball Association had a television promotion that showed players exuberantly displaying their skills. Words flashed across the TV screen as a voice proclaimed, "I LOVE THIS GAME!"

It is time for those who care about educating young people to adopt the same slogan. Let's take a break from discussion of the means of education for awhile and concentrate on how we can convince students through our deeds and words that when we gather with them in this wonderful pursuit called learning, WE LOVE THIS GAME! If we can do that, they will come in time to love this game too.

CHAPTER 7

Another Love: A Teacher's Passion for Her Discipline

Teaching is an affair of the heart, not just the intellect, as Roland Barth has pointed out in his book *Learning by Heart*. A teacher must love her students and demonstrate that love for them, but there is something else a teacher must love as well. Yes, it turns out that the teacher is involved in a love triangle. For the teacher loves not only her students but the subject(s) she teaches. Fortunately, the teacher doesn't have to keep her other love a secret; in fact, the teacher is most effective when she openly acknowledges her passion for that other love.

Have you ever had a teacher who made a subject come alive for you and made you hungry for more and more of it? What was it that the teacher did that sparked your enthusiasm for that subject? Take a minute and think about that. It is not a frivolous question. It cuts to the heart of what inspirational teachers do and what mediocre ones fail to do.

The most common answer to that question is that the inspiring teacher made her consuming passion for her discipline so palpable in a classroom that that passion ignited a similar passion for the subject in students.

Recently I asked students in a graduate class I was teaching if they had ever had a teacher who got them excited about a subject they did not think they'd like and what the teacher did to spark that excitement. This paraphrased response given by one of the students is typical of what you often hear about inspiring teachers.

> When I had teachers I could tell weren't excited about what they were teaching and did not want to be there, it was much more difficult to learn. I remember I had a class in my undergraduate years that I was not excited about. When I went to class on the first day, my professor jumped right into the work by showing us paintings and architecture and the passion he had for the subject. I was always

excited to go to this class because I knew I would always learn something new and thought provoking.

A teacher influences the lives of students by helping them love what they are learning—not just love it enough to get them into university or a good job, but to love it for all the other things it can bring to their lives, including the sheer joy of learning for learning's sake. In T. H. White's *The Once and Future King*, Merlyn tells his pupil, the future King Arthur:

> The best thing for being sad . . . is to learn something. That is the only thing that never fails. You may grow old and trembling in your anatomies, you may lie awake at night listening to the disorder of your veins, you may miss your only love, you may see the world about you devastated by evil lunatics, or know your honour trampled in the sewers of baser minds. There is only one thing for it then—to learn. Learn why the world wags and what wags it. That is the only thing which the mind can never exhaust, never alienate, never be tortured by, never fear or distrust, and never dream of regretting. (1965, p. 183)

In *Practicing History*, historian Barbara Tuchman described two teachers whose love for their disciplines made an indelible impression on her. The first was historian C. H. McIlwain. Another was her literature professor, John Livingston Lowes. Notice the effect his passion has on her. Imagine what you could accomplish if your passion had a similar effect on your students.

> John Livingston Lowe's English 72 . . . included his spectacular tour de force on the origins of "The Ancient Mariner" and "Kubla Khan." He waved at Wordsworth, bowed briefly to Keats and Shelley and really let himself go through twelve weeks of lectures, tracing the sources of Coleridge's imagery, spending a week on the fatal apparition of the person from Porlock. What kept us, at least me, on the edge of my seat throughout this exploit was Lowe's *enthusiasm for his subject*. (1981, p. 14; emphasis added)

Great teachers, like great artists, great athletes, or great scientists, are much more than merely masters of what they do—they are lovers of what they do. In fact, their love for what they are teaching is, in part, what has helped them become masters in the first place. While a student might occasionally admire a teacher's teaching technique, it is the teacher's passion that inevitably takes a student in thrall and keeps him enthralled long after a course has been completed.

Teachers who are in love with a discipline teach students that learning is enjoyable, and they teach that by displaying their own delight in what they are teaching. Many who talk about education these days are fond of promoting the notion of "academic rigor" as the most important element of an education.

While rigor should be part of the process of learning, overemphasis on it makes a classroom sterile, leeching the vitality out of it and turning what should be a lively encounter with knowledge into an experience as appealing as a trip to the dentist. Remember, words determine not only how we think but how we act. That's why academic "vigor" is a better goal for teachers to pursue than academic "rigor."

Inspirational teachers don't teach their students that learning is fun by lecturing about how enjoyable it can be; they teach it like John Livingston Lowes did, by displaying their own excitement about it.

A teacher's love for her discipline isn't just a "nice" but somewhat superfluous quality; it is an essential attribute. Without it a teacher's teaching techniques, or even her love for students, no matter how refined they may be, become mundane. With it . . . Well, I'll let Barbara Tuchman tell you:

> Although I did not know it or formulate it consciously at the time, it is this quality of being in love with your subject that is indispensable for writing good history—or good anything for that matter. (1981, p. 15)

So whenever anyone asks "What's love got to do with it?," don't hesitate to tell them.

CHAPTER 8

Discipline: The Gift of Love

Talk about love in relation to learning and teaching and some people think you are an educational sissy, one of those warm and fuzzy freaks who wants to spoil kids and doesn't have a clue about such things as "academic rigor."

I'll admit that I don't much like the term "academic rigor." It has too much rigidity about it. There's harshness even in the sound of the words that puts me off. I think academic "vigor" is a much more suitable objective to strive for than academic "rigor."

Some will, of course, see this distinction as mere semantic waffling, but it is not. Vigor, with its connotation of energy and vitality, is a more inspiring goal to strive for than rigor. People, including young people, are more motivated to pursue excellence when they feel the challenge is dynamic and invigorating.

At the same time, I want to be clear that the love I'm talking about in this book isn't all warm and cuddly like a teddy bear. At times, as warm and cuddly as our love may need to be, the love I'm talking about is demanding when the situation calls for it. Sometimes students, to put it bluntly, need a loving boot in the butt to get them going. There is a big difference, though, between a boot in the butt and a loving boot in the butt, and most youngsters understand that difference—even when they pretend not to.

Early in my teaching career, I shared a classroom with a teacher with many years of experience behind her. She turned out to be a terrific mentor in many ways.

One afternoon after first-quarter report cards had been handed out, we were in the classroom reviewing our day when a student stormed into the room. He made straight for the teacher's desk where we were talking. When he reached it, he slammed his report card onto the desk and shouted, "I want to thank you, Mrs. Martin [not her real name] for the *F* you gave me."

Mrs. Martin picked up the report card and calmly handed it back to him. "No need to thank me, Robert. You've earned it."

I remember how impressed I was with Mrs. Martin's poise under pressure. It wasn't until a couple of weeks after the incident that I discovered an even greater reason to admire her.

One afternoon after school, I was walking by the school library and happened to glance in. There was Mrs. Martin sitting at a table working with Robert. I learned later that he'd come to her and apologized and told her he needed help to pull his grade up to a passing grade. Mrs. Martin gladly obliged.

Robert, as I recall, eventually got a B in English that year, and I can assure you, he earned it. That's what a loving boot in the butt can do.

When you ask a young person "What is discipline?" invariably you get the same reply—"Punishment." Not infrequently, you get a similar response from adults. This may explain why so few youngsters welcome discipline and why so many adults feel uncomfortable when they have to administer it. If discipline is punishment, who needs it?

But discipline has really gotten a bad rap. While punishment is one of its many definitions, it is by no means the primary one. In *Webster's New World Dictionary of the American Language* (1968), it is the last one, reluctantly squeezed in there with all those other definitions that have to do with teaching, training, and the development of personal control. The word "discipline" actually comes from the Latin root word meaning "to learn." It's a close relative of the word "disciple," meaning "pupil" or "learner."

How can a caring adult discipline in such a way that it is viewed by young people as a constructive part of their growth and development? How can he get students to see it as a positive rather than a negative? How can he use it to enhance their learning? In other words, how can teaching adults convince students that, rather than being punishment, discipline is a gift of love? These are questions we must ask ourselves *before* we discipline youngsters.

Our actions must match our intention and show students that the purpose of discipline is not to give *us* control over their lives but rather to give it to them.

When discipline is most effective, it teaches young people that they must develop self-control in order to be truly independent. It helps them see how undisciplined individuals, such as alcoholics, drug addicts, and individuals given to fits of anger or other bad habits, are not really independent but rather dependent on their out-of-control behaviors. It teaches them how developing self-discipline helps people—athletes, soldiers, musicians, and even us—to perform better in the tasks, personal and professional, we have to do. That is why our discipline must result from reflection rather than impulse.

Helping a youngster develop good discipline demands that we allow a youngster to learn there are consequences that result from his lack of discipline. This is the tough part of our love, but it's just as important as the tender part. Failure to teach young people to accept the consequences of lack of discipline or shying away from giving them consequences for misbehavior isn't love, it's neglect—the kind of neglect that can cost a young person dearly in later life. Getting this part of teaching discipline right is no easy task, and even the best of intentions can end in failure.

When I was six years old, my mother disciplined me for repeating a "purple" expression I'd learned in the schoolyard. The approach she chose was feeding me a tablespoon of hot mustard when I repeated the word to her. To this day, I still occasionally curse, but I don't ever touch mustard if I can avoid it. And that's the truth.

My mother's intentions were good, but in this case, the lesson I learned from her discipline was muddied by a poorly chosen consequence. A discipliner must carefully consider the consequence that should follow misbehavior before applying it. If a youngster cannot see a clear connection between his action and the consequence, he may learn the wrong lesson.

In one high school where I served as principal, a group of students on a three-day field trip were discovered drinking by a faculty chaperone doing a room check before lights-out. Adolescents consuming alcohol on a school trip is a serious offense in any school and usually results in suspension. Indeed, the trip chaperones and I did consider a three-day suspension as a possible consequence of the students' drinking.

But we decided to take a day to think over what consequence would best teach students the lesson we wanted them to learn about the seriousness of their behavior. In the end, we came to the consensus that rather than assume a three-day out-of-school suspension would teach the students what they really needed to learn about drinking and breaking school rules, we'd take a different approach.

The half-dozen students involved received a one-day in-school suspension. On that day, they were given an assignment that required them to review our school's five core values, with emphasis on two of them—*respect for all* and *sense of self*. (See appendix 2 for the school's mission statement and core values.) They were to prepare themselves to discuss how they had violated these values.

The assignment required that they research alcoholism and how quickly an adolescent, compared to an adult, could become alcoholic. A third part of the assignment sent the students to interview each of the six chaperones who had taken time away from their families to take their classes on the trip. The students had to find out how these faculty members felt about their behavior.

Finally, the offenders had to discuss and come to consensus about strategies they would use to avoid drinking during school events in the future. That wasn't the end of the consequence, though. There was one more stage.

On the following day after school, the students gave a group presentation on what they had researched the day before. The panel discussion was attended by their parents, the trip chaperones, and me, the principal. All of us had a rubric that we used to assess the quality of the students' presentation.

In the end, the quality of the students' research was excellent, and although a couple (due to nervousness, no doubt) could have done a better job of presenting, it was clear to everyone in attendance that these students really did understand what they had done wrong, why it was such a concern for us, and how they had disappointed their parents, teachers, and other members of the school community.

When we teach young people that they must develop self-discipline and we help them to do it, we give them a precious gift that will serve them well for a lifetime.

Finally, we must consider this before we leave this subject. Sometimes when we discipline, the best strategy may be to accent the positive rather than highlighting the negative, as the following story illustrates.

A father was trying to cure his teenage son of cursing. He sat the boy down one day and said, "Son, as you grow older, using that kind of language is going to cause you problems in life. So in order to help you overcome your cursing, I've come up with a plan.

"I bought this bucket of spikes and a hammer from the hardware store. I'm going to put the bucket and the hammer on the back porch. Now, you see that big oak tree in our backyard? Every time I hear you swearing, I'm going to ask you to go take a spike out of that bucket and hammer it into the trunk of that oak as a reminder of the behavior you have to eliminate. Agree?" The son agreed.

A month later, the father happened to glance up from his morning coffee and noticed that the trunk of the oak was almost completely covered with spikes. That afternoon, he sat his son down and acknowledged the error of his strategy.

"Son, I apologize. We've been using the wrong approach in dealing with your problem. We're going to take a different approach. Every time I notice that you've gone half a day without using one of those expressions, I'm going to send you out there to take one of those spikes out of that oak tree. Agree?" The son agreed.

A few months later when the father looked out at the oak tree, he noticed that almost all of the spikes were gone.

Saint Paul wrote, "No discipline seems pleasant at the time, but painful. Later on, however, it produces a harvest of righteousness and peace for those who have been trained by it" (Hebrews 12:11).

That is why discipline, lovingly applied and properly chosen, is a gift of love rather than a punishment.

PRINCIPLES OF GOOD DISCIPLINE

- Discipline without anger, even if you have to wait awhile until your anger is under control. Refer to the disciplinary actions you take as "consequences" rather than "punishment."
- Help the disciplined youngster process what happened and why, and then work with her to develop a plan to address the problem so it doesn't reoccur.
- Avoid inconsistency—addressing a behavior one time and allowing it to pass at another time because you are too busy.
- Resist the urge not to discipline because you feel sorry for a youngster. You can empathize with how a youngster is feeling about the mistake he made, but letting him escape the consequences of his action is a mistake you don't want to make.
- Separate the deed from the doer in your own mind and in the mind of the offender. It is not uncommon for a student you are disciplining to feel that because of what she has done, you don't like her. Make it clear that it is her action you cannot accept, not her.
- Make the point with a youngster clearly and concisely. If you go on and on, a youngster will learn to tune you out. Deaf ears do not respond well to correction.
- Catch a youngster who has been disciplined being good (regularly) and acknowledge it. A carrot is a better motivator than the stick and healthier too.

QUESTIONS FIELD TRIP STUDENTS WERE EXPECTED TO ADDRESS

- Which of the school's core values have you violated by your actions, and in what ways have you violated them? (Be specific in your answer. A general statement that you shouldn't be drinking will not be acceptable.)
- In what ways have you disappointed your parents, your chaperones, your fellow trip members, the school community, and yourself?

- What does research say about teenage drinking and alcoholism?
- If you were again confronted with the opportunity to drink on another trip, what *specific strategies* would you use to keep yourself and your fellow students from doing it?
- What is the most important lesson that you have learned from this experience?

CHAPTER 9

Bringing "Awesome" Back into the Classroom

"Awesome!" Years ago this was one of the most overused words in an adolescent's vocabulary. Young people used it to describe everything, including an occasional school experience. The word became, for me, a colorless cliché, but now that I don't hear it much anymore, I admit I miss it. The word conveys high excitement, the type of excitement that young people feel when they encounter something wonderful—something that inspires *wonder*. We would do well to bring "awesome" back into the classroom. How can we do that?

Let's begin with how not to do it. Consider Walt Whitman's "When I Heard the Learn'd Astronomer" as a warning label on an instructional practice that dulls rather than inspires *awe*some.

When I heard the learn'd astronomer;
When the proofs, the figures, were ranged in columns before me;
When I was shown the charts and the diagrams, to add, divide, and measure them;
When I, sitting, heard the astronomer, where he lectured with much applause in
the lecture-room,
How soon, unaccountable, I became tired and sick;
Till rising and gliding out, I wander'd off by myself,
In the mystical moist night-air, and from time to time,
Look'd up in perfect silence at the stars. (Miller 1959, p. 196)

Whitman's poem describes an all too common teaching practice that deadens the wonder that is essential for engaging students in a learning experience: beginning a lesson with an abstract learning activity, like a lecture or textbook reading, rather than a concrete one. Whitman is a poet, but you could easily find similar warnings about this toxic pedagogy from historians, researchers, psychologists, and scientists.

Return with me for a few minutes to Whitman's poem, and let's examine how he captures what is least awesome about so many classroom learning experiences in literature, mathematics, social studies, science, or any other subject. Read the poem again, slowly.

Notice the repetition of *when, when, when* and how this repetition and the length of the lines indicate an increasing tiresomeness with the lecture? Does it remind you of any of the classroom lectures you've attended—or given? Read what the poet does once he has escaped from the lecture hall:

> Till rising and gliding out, I wander'd off by myself,
> In the mystical moist night-air, and from time to time,
> Look'd up in perfect silence at the stars.

That look isn't just a look—it is an expression of "awesome."

Well, what could the astronomer have done to make his presentation awesome? Like most students if we were to ask them, Whitman also is able to offer an answer.

Suppose the astronomer had taken his class outside and given his lecture under the stars where students could see the marvels he was describing. Imagine the effect if he had begun his presentation by encouraging his students to look up at the stars and express their emotional response to them. Consider the class's reaction if he had invited them to think about questions that rose up in their minds as they looked up at the stars.

What might he have achieved if instead of using charts and graphs and diagrams, he had used the starscape itself to make his points? What might have been the outcome of the lecture if the astronomer had talked about mistaken ideas that people, including scientists, once held about the stars? What might have been the impact had he described the efforts of scientists who were trying to unravel those still unsolved mysteries of the stars and if he had encouraged his class to try to solve some of the mysteries themselves? How might they have responded if he had reminded them that like them, astronomers are people who wonder about the stars? Might he have stirred the imaginations of his audience and heard some voices cry "Awesome"?

The problem with so many classroom learning experiences, like the one Whitman described, is that they insist on introducing students to new concepts through abstract learning activities instead of concrete ones. While students can learn something from abstract learning activities, it is through concrete encounters with what they must learn that students experience awe and a desire to learn more.

Teachers should begin teaching a new concept by introducing students to something tangible or mysterious about it and having them wonder about it before beginning any lecture or having them read about it in a textbook.

Textbooks in particular can have a carcinogenic effect on learning because in addition to being written in a style that is passionless, they insist on thrusting students, even very young ones, into abstractions before they have had a chance to experience something tangibly and emotionally.

In *The Pleasure of Finding Things Out*, Nobel Prize–winning physicist Richard Feynman described this all-too-common problem with a textbook approach to trying to teach students new concepts. He cited a first-grade science book that showed a picture of a wind-up toy dog and asked, "What makes it move?" The answer the book was looking for is that "energy makes it move." Feynman took exception with this approach, saying it begins in the wrong place.

Instead, he said, when confronted with the question "What makes it move?" the student should be told, "Open it up; let's look at it." Definitions of energy and explanations about how energy works must come later, after the child has had a chance to experience the intricacy of the springs and gears that make the toy move (Feynman 1999, pp. 178–79)—in other words, after the child has looked inside at the springs and gears and thought, "Awesome, I wonder what makes those things work like that?"

With a little imagination, we can bring "awesome" back into the classroom, no matter what subject we teach.

I watched a middle school special education teacher introduce the concept of fractions to her students by having them stand up and get into a straight line and then divide that line in half, then quarters, then eighths, and so forth. Then she had them recombine the various fractions until they were one line again. In this way, she gave students the physical look and "feel" for what adding and dividing fractions was all about.

When I taught high school English, I introduced my students to Robert Frost's "Mending Wall" and its theme of separation and alienation by giving them as a weekend homework assignment the task of locating a stone wall and either taking a photo of it or making a sketch of it.

I asked them to record in their journals any impressions they had about the wall they had chosen. I developed a series of questions for them to consider: How does this wall make you feel when you look at it? What questions come to mind as you look at it? Does the location of the wall raise any questions in your mind? What condition is the wall in? If it needs repair, who do you suppose repairs it and when? What do you suppose the purpose of this wall is or was? The questions were merely prompts. I told students to use them only if they felt they needed them.

When students entered class on Monday morning, they noticed that my desk was enclosed by a wall constructed from cardboard and chimney paper. From behind my desk, I was invisible to them. And that's what I wanted.

I instructed students to take the piece of tape that was on each desk and use it to attach their wall pictures to the wall around my desk. I gave them a few minutes to quietly review their journal entries about their walls. When they had finished, I introduced them to Frost's poem.

I taught the entire lesson from behind my wall. It made the students uneasy (not to mention me). Several students pleaded with me to come out from behind my wall because they were so uncomfortable with the physical separation between us.

By the end of the class, my students had a "feel" for why Frost said in his poem, "Something there is that doesn't love a wall" and "Before I built a wall I'd ask to know/What I was walling in and walling out." In subsequent classes, we had lively discussions about my wall, the wall in Frost's poem, the Great Wall of China, the Berlin Wall, the Iron Curtain, and the invisible walls that people sometimes put up to separate themselves from other people. And, of course, about the power of metaphor. It was "awesome."

Learning was never meant to be the dreary encounter that is detailed in Whitman's poem and that is too often the experience of so many students today. Any teacher, using a little imagination, can create lessons that are engaging and inspiring.

So as you get ready to introduce that new lesson, remember Whitman's experience with the uninspiring astronomer, and don't force your students to endure a similar experience. Instead, think about what you can do to create a learning activity that will capture students' imaginations and inspire them to wonder. When you succeed, don't be surprised if you hear them say, "This is awesome."

Ah, what a lovely expression that is when you hear it in a classroom!

CHAPTER 10

Restoring Joy to Learning

In 1965, Richard Feynman won a Nobel Prize for his work in quantum electrodynamics. Now quantum electrodynamics is pretty heady stuff. Feynman's work involved difficult mathematics, complex technical problem solving, and painstaking experimentation that took years of dedicated work to complete. So one might be tempted to listen to a man like him when he talks about learning and what it takes to succeed in it.

What he has to say is really quite remarkable, perhaps even disconcerting, especially for those who rail about the need for more "academic rigor" in schools. When Feynman speaks about learning, his words are not about rigor or discipline or about beating others in a competition for academic excellence—they are about joy.

In 1981, on the BBC program *Horizon*, when he was asked was it (his work on quantum electrodynamics) worth the Nobel Prize, he responded:

> I don't see that it makes any point that someone in the Swedish Academy decides that this work is noble enough to receive a prize. I've already got the prize. The prize is the pleasure of finding the thing out, the kick in the discovery, the observation that other people use it [my work]. Those are the real things. The honors are unreal to me. (Feynman 1999, p. 12)

This was not the only time Feynman emphasized the importance of joy in learning. In a speech he gave to fellow scientists in Hawaii he made the point again:

> Another value of science is the fun called intellectual enjoyment which some people get from reading and learning and thinking about it, and which others get from working in it. This is an important point, one which is not considered enough by those who tell us it is our social responsibility to reflect on the impact of science on society. (Feynman 1999, p. 143)

Feynman's comments are a reminder of what we should, but so seldom do, emphasize in schools. Learning is supposed to be enjoyable, and there is nothing wrong with that.

In fact, if there isn't a large element of joy in learning, that's a signal that something is wrong and that what we are doing in our classrooms warrants serious examination. No, not that kind of examination; we have enough of that kind. The examination I'm talking about is self-examination, coupled with faculty discussion about what may be interfering with the joy of learning in a school.

In *A Place Called School*, John Goodlad wrote that the one thousand classrooms he and his team had visited were

> almost completely devoid of outward evidences of affect. Shared laughter, overt enthusiasm, or angry outbursts were rarely observed. Less than 3 percent of classroom time was devoted to praise, abrasive comments, expressions of joy or humor, or somewhat unbridled outbursts such as "wow" or "great." (1984, pp. 229–30)

Every educator should be dismayed by that discovery. Goodlad made that observation back in 1984 before *A Nation at Risk*, No Child Left Behind, and Race to the Top had a chance to throw vinegar on the idea that learning should be joyful.

It's time for us to reevaluate our commitment to a Spartan approach to teaching and learning and replace it with one that seeks to emphasize the lighter side of learning—the joyous, the playful, the pleasurable side of it.

Oh, I recognize that if we do that, we will have to engage the educational militarists who believe any emphasis on joy in learning will turn students into academic sissies. On the other hand, if business guru Tom Peters can write a book titled *The Pursuit of Wow!* and a Noble Prize–winning physicist can title a collection of his work *The Pleasure of Finding Things Out*, we've got some heady (pun intended) support to help us make the case for a new approach.

What can you do to restore the joy of learning in your classroom?

RECOVER YOUR OWN JOY AND SHARE IT

Begin by rediscovering (if you've lost or forgotten it) your own joy in learning. You can't share what you don't have. Reflect on the joy you experienced when you were first learning the subject you now teach. Recall the delight you experienced when you first became a teacher. Read a book in which someone describes his delight in learning; it will help you to revive your own. I mention several of these books at the end of this chapter.

Watch a movie about an inspiring teacher and see how she finds pleasure in what she is doing. You'll find some movie suggestions at the end of this chapter as well. If you keep a journal, go back and read over your moments of enjoyable learning.

Once you have started to recover your own joy, or if you've never lost it, bring it into the classroom. Make it visible. Talk about the fun of learning, the pleasure of discovery, the satisfaction of learning to do something well. Talk about it often when specific occasions for joy occur, not just once at the beginning of a school year. Speak with passion and enthusiasm. Don't preach, but share your enthusiasm and don't be afraid to use words like "wow" and "awesome" and "that's great." When you use a joyful expression, mean it.

CREATE LEARNING ACTIVITIES THAT EXCITE STUDENTS' CURIOSITY AND IMAGINATION

We've all heard the expression "curiosity killed the cat." It's a terrible expression. It discourages curiosity instead of encouraging it. I suppose there have been occasions on which curiosity has killed a cat or two, but they don't match the mortality rate that lack of curiosity has on classroom learning. Remember the teacher I described in chapter 2, who had the Take-Apart Corner? He knew how to provoke curiosity. Remember my students' reaction to my being behind the wall that surrounded my desk? You can believe they were curious about what I was up to.

Once you have roused students' curiosity, use it to spur their imaginations and creativity. During one class, years ago, a colleague I was team-teaching with brought a Venus flytrap to class and showed students how it captured flies. That demonstration prepared them for an assignment we were about to give them. The assignment was for each student to design a mousetrap that would capture a mouse without killing it. My colleague was teaching students about synectics and how scientists and inventors often use what they observe in nature as a means of creating a product or solving a problem.

In each of the previous situations, the teacher's curiosity was as much a factor as the students'. That fourth-grade teacher loved to take mechanical things apart; he was sharing that love with his students. My colleague introduced the class to synectics because it was one of his favorite problem-solving approaches. I was highly curious and excited about what effect my being behind a wall would have on my students.

"When I examine myself and my methods of thought," wrote Albert Einstein, "I come to the conclusion that the gift of fantasy has meant more to me than any talent for abstract, positive thinking" (www.brainyquote.com/quotes/quotes/a/alberteins133826.html).

HAVE FUN WITH YOUR KIDS

I am by no means a stand-up comedian, but when I found myself getting too somber about my responsibilities as a teacher or principal, I'd remind myself to get out and have some fun with the kids. As a teacher, when the lesson was done, I'd sometimes end with a question for the class, something like this:

Mr. Connolly is the older brother of what famous movie star?
a. Tom Cruise
b. Mel Gibson
c. Leonardo DiCaprio
d. the actor who plays Freddy in *Friday the 13th*

As a middle school principal, I'd tell new students and their parents that we had an intelligence test that we gave to all new students at the end of the year. They had to pass it to go on to the next grade. I'd tell them the intelligence test had only one question, a very challenging one. I'd embellish the difficulty by telling them that some kids, and even some teachers, had been retained in the same grade for years because they couldn't correctly answer the question. Then I'd give them the question, "Who is the greatest middle school principal in the cosmic universe?"

The most fun, of course, came when kids got the joke and didn't give me the answer they thought would flatter me. The point wasn't to convince everybody that I was a great comedian; it was to remind me and them that school can be fun. Find your own ways to enjoy and have fun with students.

EMPHASIZE THAT PLEASURE LIES IN THE PROCESS OF LEARNING, NOT JUST IN ITS PRODUCT

We are such a product-oriented society that we lose sight of the pleasure in the process of learning. Artist Julia Cameron pointed out an obvious but oft-forgotten fact in her book *The Artist's Way*: "'I am writing a screenplay' is infinitely more interesting to the soul than 'I've written a screenplay,' which pleases the ego. 'I am in an acting class' is infinitely more interesting than 'I took an acting class a few years ago'" (2002, p. 139).

So it is with all captivating learning experiences; the delight resides in the process more than it does in the end product. That's good news for all of us who genuinely love learning because it assures us that there need be no end to the thing we love. There may be peaks and prizes along the way, but the kick is always in discovering new aspects and new depths in what we are learning—and that is a reward worth having.

Introducing the idea of the joy in learning into our classrooms will not destroy a classroom's capacity for academic rigor; it will only enhance it. When we enjoy what we are doing, whatever it may be, we are more willing to work harder to meet the challenges that pursuit poses. Just ask an athlete, an artist, or, for that matter, a Noble Prize–winning physicist.

READINGS DESCRIBING THE JOYS OF LEARNING

The Artist's Way: A Spiritual Path to Higher Creativity, by Julia Cameron (an excellent book that describes how individuals can discover or recover the joy of writing or other artistic pursuits)

The Pleasure of Finding Things Out: The Best Short Works of Richard P. Feynman, by Richard Feynman (a collection of Feynman's essays; read especially "The Pleasure of Finding Things Out," "What Is Science?" and "The Value of Science")

OTHER READINGS RELATED TO THE JOY OF LEARNING

Hard Times, by Charles Dickens (describes what happens when learning is joyless and strictly utilitarian)

The Demon-Haunted World: Science as a Candle in the Dark, by Carl Sagan (read his description of his own joyless experience of learning science in middle and high school)

Small Is Beautiful: Economics as if People Mattered, by E. F. Schumacher

"When I Heard the Learn'd Astronomer," in *Leaves of Grass*, by Walt Whitman (Whitman's short poem about how to anesthetize learners)

MOVIES THAT CELEBRATE THE JOY OF LEARNING

Dead Poets Society
The Karate Kid
Stand and Deliver
To Sir, with Love
Mr. Holland's Opus
Freedom Writers
The Emperor's Club

CHAPTER 11

When Learning Isn't Fun

Learning isn't always fun. At times it is just plain hard work. Remember those days when you had to spend hours struggling to master some new information or a new skill? Remember as a kid sitting at your desk in your room or at the kitchen table, ankle deep in wads of crumpled-up paper, the discarded refuse of unfinished attempts at completing an assignment due the following day? Remember the broken or twisted remains of pencils and pens that lay on your desk or on the floor, ghastly reminders of the destruction that frustration can produce?

Can you recall that distraught voice that cried from the back of your mind, "I can't do it; it's too hard," or that sense of anxiety, that feeling that you weren't quite up to the task, that maybe you weren't smart enough or gifted enough? Now, remember the breakthroughs, those moments when, after persistent effort, it finally came out right? EUREKA, I'VE GOT IT!

Those were the magic moments when you experienced that wonderful sense of accomplishment and the joy it brings, moments of self-discovery when you learned the value of determination. The victories weren't always assured, and that's what made them particularly satisfying when they came. Isn't that the way it should be? Isn't that what learning is all about—effort (sometimes extraordinary effort) that results in intellectual growth?

Test pilots have an expression for going beyond the limits of what they are sure they can do. They call it "pushing the edge of the envelope." When we give students assignments that truly challenge them, pushing them beyond their comfort level, that is what we are teaching them—that they must learn to push the edges of their cognitive and emotional envelopes. It's a good lesson, and a necessary one, but it isn't necessarily an enjoyable experience for them—at least in the beginning.

In physical exercise, students easily agree with the notion of "no pain, no gain." In academic pursuits, it is harder for them to accept that idea, but it is no less important that they do. Whenever we stretch, truly stretch (no pseudo-stretching allowed), either physically or intellectually, we should expect some discomfort, even pain—but we can expect growth and gain as well. Thomas Edison told his protégés that "genius" was 5 percent inspiration and 95 percent perspiration.

When researchers tackled the task of isolating the characteristics of success-ful people, they found that these people possessed many characteristics that were different from one individual to the next but that all successful people had two things in common: belief in their own abilities and the capacity to work hard and persist.

Teachers who are determined to educate students to love learning teach them to believe in themselves and in their ability to endure when the task is difficult. (Remember Mrs. Martin and Robert?) A teacher who genuinely cares about her students knows that challenge is what they need to become strong, capable, confident learners. Facing a difficult challenge isn't generally a com-fortable experience for students, nor is it painless for those who must watch them struggle with it, but the reward when the challenge is met successfully is worth it for both.

In my office hangs a poster of a runner facing a long stretch of uphill ter-rain. He can see the road uphill laid out for miles ahead of him. One can only imagine what *he's* thinking, but the caption reads, "The race is not always to the swift, but to those who keep on running." That lesson is what the effective teacher teaches students.

Yes, the math, the science, the history, and the writing skills we teach are important, but we must never forget that the roads individuals take to knowledge and understanding will at times test the limits of their character and endurance. So compassionate educators teach students that while the learning challenge they are currently facing may not be fun, they will experi-ence a sense of satisfaction, perhaps even joy, once they have successfully completed it.

Many youngsters become easily discouraged and are inclined to give up when they meet with difficulty, not to mention failure. They lack conviction that hard work and effort (with support and occasional assistance from oth-ers) will help them prevail. These young people believe that natural ability is the only thing that makes individuals successful in life. Consequently, when they don't immediately succeed, they are inclined to doubt that they have the "natural ability" with which to pursue success in that area.

But let's not be too critical of young people in this regard. As John Gardner pointed out, this kind of doubt pursues most of us throughout our lives:

> By middle age most of us carry in our heads a tremendous catalogue of things we have no intention of trying again because we tried them once and failed—or tried them once and did less well than our self-esteem demanded. (1995, p. 14)

Other students are intimidated by the success of their parents. They look at their parents and see them as having sprung into being competent from the very start—another manifestation of the "natural ability" belief. One day our daughter, in frustration, shouted at her mother, "Well, of course, I'll never be as good as you at understanding people. You've always been good at it."

She wasn't being flippant. She believed, at that stage of her life, that understanding people was a gift granted by the gods rather than a skill developed through practice. Youngsters seldom know the challenges we adults have had to overcome, the failures we've had to endure to gain our measure of success—unless we tell them. Even then they may find it hard to believe.

Adults committed to helping students develop a love of learning need to address youngsters' misconceptions about what is required for success in learning. They need to teach kids to keep on trying when they are confronted with a challenge that doesn't yield easily to success. Young people must learn that frustration and setbacks are only temporary stumbling blocks along the way to eventual success for those who are willing to persevere. If we neglect to teach students this critical lesson, they will likely pay a heavy price in the future.

> We pay a heavy price for our fear of failure. It is a powerful obstacle to growth. It assures the progressive narrowing of the personality and prevents exploration and experimentation. There is no learning without some difficulty and fumbling. If you want to keep on learning, you must keep on risking failure—all your life. It's as simple as that. (Gardner 1995, p. 15)

When learning isn't fun but hard work, giving encouragement to a youngster, especially one who is struggling and feeling discouraged, isn't always easy. Well-intentioned advice or encouragement can easily end up as ineffectual dialogue (or worse, monologue). Here are a few suggestions for encouraging students through those times when learning isn't fun. Don't restrict yourself to just those listed. Reflect on other ways you might help youngsters through their periods of struggle.

- Talk about your own struggles as you faced difficult learning challenges. Talk about the emotions you felt as you faced those challenges and how you had to learn to deal with your feelings of "I don't know if I can do this." Especially, don't forget to mention your feelings when you eventually achieved success.

- Listen carefully when a youngster is disappointed or discouraged and needs to talk. Give a youngster the opportunity to discuss how he *feels* about the things that are discouraging him. Often what you have to address is the feeling rather than provide a solution to the problem.

- Put up posters around your classroom or home that specifically deal with the issues of failure and discouragement. Here are two examples: "Success consists of going from failure to failure without loss of enthusiasm" (Winston Churchill). "It's like learning to ski. If you're not falling down, you're not learning" (William D. Smithburg, former president and CEO of Quaker Oats Company).

- Model picking yourself up and moving on after having been flattened by failure or disappointment. If you are an English teacher and a writer like me, bring in some of your rejection letters and read them to students, but make sure you bring in some of your published work as well.

- Have students read about people who have overcome failure and disappointment and eventually achieved success: Washington at Valley Forge, Bell and Edison in their laboratories, Margaret Mead in Samoa, or Florence Nightingale during the Crimean War. Include stories of some of your students' sports or entertainment heroes as well.

- Encourage a youngster to continue to "try" despite disappointment or failure. Don't let a youngster view failure as final. Model your own willingness to accept encouragement from others, including children, when you need it.

Those times when learning isn't fun often provide a teacher with his most teachable moments. Don't waste time lecturing students about how learning can't always be fun, that it's sometimes just hard work. Instead, lovingly guide students through those moments of struggle, firm in the conviction that, like the rest of us, young people too will find satisfaction, even joy, when, after struggling with a difficult challenge, they eventually achieve success.

CHAPTER 12

Education Should Nourish the Spirit

Past the seeker as he prayed came the sick, the hungry, the tired and poor,
the forlorn and forsaken. And the seeker cried out in anguish, "Oh dear
God, how can you look upon such misery and not do something!" And
deep in the depth of his soul the seeker heard a voice that said: "I did do
something; I made you."

a Sufi story

Almost all the conversation we hear these days about improving schools has to do with preparing students for employment. While preparing young people for future employment is an important practical task of education, many young people today feel there is something missing in their schooling—something vital.

In 2007, speaking at Harvard's commencement, Bill Gates identified that missing something. After thanking the Harvard faculty for the many learning opportunities they had given him, Gates said, "But taking a serious look back, I do have one big regret. I left Harvard with no real awareness of the awful inequities in the world—the appalling disparities of health and wealth, and opportunity that condemn millions of people to lives of despair."

He challenged Harvard's students and faculty to use what they learned in school to "be activists. Take on the big inequities," and he promised them that doing so would be "one of the great experiences of your lives" (2007).

Young people long to contribute to society, to make it better. They don't relish having to sit and wait until adults declare them "grown up enough" to make a contribution. And why should they? If they are ready, why are we holding them back? Why are we denying them "one of the great experiences of their lives"? Why aren't we encouraging them and helping them find ways to contribute now?

The power teachers have to help students satisfy their need to make a difference in this world is great. That point was poignantly made by a student, a Global Citizenship Award winner, in a speech he gave at a conference for international teachers.

Yeon Duk Woo, who was at the time attending Saigon South International School, told the following story to an audience of over one thousand educators:

> One day a son came to see his father. He was tired and frustrated. He complained to his father about how difficult life had become for him and confessed that he just wanted to give up. His father, who was a chef, pulled up a chair for his son and invited him to sit down.
>
> When he was seated, his dad took three pots of water and placed each one on the stove. When the water came to a boil, he took a carrot and cut it up into the first pot. Into the second pot, he put an egg. And into the third, he put some ground-up coffee. After a few minutes, he said to his son, "Come on over here, son, I want to show you something."
>
> As they stood looking at the pots boiling on the stove, the father asked, "What do you see?"
>
> Impatiently the son replied, "I see three pots, one with carrots, one with an egg, and one with coffee."
>
> "Look closer," his father said. "Can't you see that when the carrots were subjected to the boiling water, they became soft. When the egg was subjected to the boiling water, it became hard. But the coffee . . . ah, son, the coffee changed the water."

Yeon Duk concluded, "Ladies and gentlemen, you are the ones who in your classrooms teach students what it means to be a global citizen. . . . You are the ones who teach us that we have the power to 'change the water.'" (This story can be located at http://centeroflifeministries.com/thoughts.htm; the original author is unknown.)

Some young people have discovered ways on their own or through social agencies such as churches, the YMCA, and community help groups to contribute, but many have yet to find a way to respond to that voice deep down in their soul that yearns to "make a difference." Schools that focus exclusively on preparing students for university and for future employment contribute to that problem.

Think for a moment of the unspoken message of most schooling. *In twelve or sixteen years, you'll get to use what you are learning here for something beyond more schooling.* How many adults, let alone youngsters, are willing to wait patiently for such a promise to be realized?

Educators can help students satisfy their unfulfilled desire for a purposeful life immediately, not in some foggy, far-off future. There are many ways they can help students do it—some large, some small, but all empowering. Here is one small example.

In 1988, when the budgets of cities and towns in Massachusetts were in dismal shape, the school board in the town in which I worked felt compelled to make dire cuts in the school budget. Among the programs scheduled to be axed was the after-school activities program for the middle school.

Many middle schoolers were incensed, and others were despondent. Rather than allow them to simply wallow in their anger and despair, a math/science teacher convinced his classes that perhaps they could do something to reverse the school board's decision.

He mobilized his students and sent them around the school building to find every leaking faucet and every toilet that refused to stop flushing. Since the school was a big, old building, there were more than a few of these. His students then used their research and math skills to calculate what this waste in water cost the town over the period of a year—and several years.

But that wasn't all. Class representatives were selected to present their findings first to me, their principal, and later to the superintendent and school board. Other class members had to put into packets data the class had developed—data that would clearly illustrate their findings to the school board and a cost-conscious public. The packets made more than a few references to water shortages around the world and to the responsibility of all nations to conserve this valuable resource.

In the end, the students presented such a convincing case that the after-school program was restored and leaking faucets and toilets were scheduled for repair. The conversation in town for weeks after that was about what a group of middle school students on an inspired mission could accomplish. Not everyone in town, of course, ended up happy with the school budget, but there were few complaints about the quality of the education middle school students were getting.

Did these middle schoolers learn that they have the power to make a difference? Need you ask?

A quality education should prepare students to lead purposeful lives, not just to make a living. Neil Postman, in *The End of Education*, wrote, "Any education that is mainly about economic utility is far too limited to be useful, and in any case, so diminishes the world that it mocks one's humanity" (1996, p. 31). Once they acknowledge this, those who teach should go about the business of providing students with learning opportunities that satisfy their spirits, as well as educate their brains.

Bill Gates heard that voice deep down in the depth of his soul telling him that he could do something about the poverty, misery, and inequities he was eventually able to see in this world. He resolved to do something about it. He and his wife, Melinda, established the Bill & Melinda Gates Foundation, dedicated to reducing inequities around the world, but he regrets that it took so long for him to recognize these inequities and to realize that he could do something about them.

How many youngsters in our schools have yet to realize they can make other people's lives better and by doing so, enrich their own? How many students in our schools are waiting for educators to show them they have the power to "change the water"?

OTHER EXAMPLES OF HOW TEACHERS EMPOWER STUDENTS

The Crosswalk

In an international school where I worked, the faculty was frustrated by students' failure to get to and from physical education classes on time. The general feeling was that students were dallying at their lockers and in the corridors between classes.

After a discussion of this issue with students in their classes, a student came to my office and explained that he believed the problem was not caused by students dallying in the corridors but by the fact that students had to take a circuitous route to the gym because a shorter route, which had originally been planned when the school was first built, had never been completed. I suggested that he research how much time would be saved if the shorter route had been completed.

That weekend, with the help of his father, he completed the research. He presented his findings to me the following Monday. His assessment of the problem was accurate. When we finished the construction of the shorter route to the gym, the tardiness to class diminished significantly.

Adopting an Orphanage

At an international school in Ho Chi Minh City, Vietnam, a teacher organized the student body around an effort to help a struggling orphanage. That effort started small but ended up with students raising funds to build a modern kitchen for the orphanage. In addition, every year, students from the international school and the orphanage meet for an afternoon of games and cultural activities that bond both groups together in friendship.

At that same school, a student convinced her church in the United States to provide funds for a heart transplant for a Vietnamese child. The fundraising effort was a success and so was the heart transplant. Another student convinced a group of international businessmen to provide funds so she and student volunteers she had recruited could fly to Korea during their spring break to help clean up an oil spill.

In case you haven't made the connection yet, Yeon Duk Woo studied at that same school.

Habitat for Humanity

I've worked in three schools, one in the United States and two overseas, in which teachers have involved students in working with Habitat for Humanity building homes for the poor. This has always been a rewarding and inspiring activity for the students and teachers who participated in it.

Rischard's Global Problems

On a worldwide scale, a number of schools have had their students read Jean-François Rischard's *High Noon: Twenty Global Problems, Twenty Years to Solve Them* and had them pick one of these issues they would like to work toward solving. For more about Challenge 20/20, go to www.nais.org/global/index.cfm?ItemNumber=147262&sn.ItemNumber=148035 or www.earcosgin.ning.com.

Do you have students who look around them and see so much that needs to be changed in the world but haven't yet found a way to respond to that voice deep down in their souls that is telling them, "I did do something; I made you"? Well, what are you waiting for? Start now. Show them some of the ways they too can "change the water."

CHAPTER 13

When Education Fails to Nourish the Spirit

In the last chapter, I talked about the need for an education that nourishes the spirit and looked at a few examples of what can happen when students get opportunities that do nourish their spirits.

Now, let's take a look at an example of an education that is so focused on "economic utility" that it "diminishes the world" and "mocks one's humanity." What effect does an education like that have on a student? Here's an up-close-and-personal look at that through the words of someone you may recognize.

American author John Cheever attended a prep school in Massachusetts from which he was expelled for failure to maintain good grades. He wrote about the experience years later in a story he titled "Expelled." What he had to say about his sad school experience should give all who love learning and want students to love it too pause because it resonates with truth even to this day.

> It was not the fault of the school at all. It was the fault of the system—the non-educational system, the college-preparatory system. That was what made the school so useless.
>
> As a college-preparatory school it was a fine school. In five years they could make raw material look like college material. They could clothe it and breed it and make it say the right things when the colleges asked it to talk. That was its duty.
>
> They weren't prepared to educate anybody. They were members of a college-preparatory system. No one around there wanted to be educated. No sir. (Cavitch 1983, pp. 183–84)

In this story, Cheever exonerates the school's headmaster and faculty for their failure to nourish his spirit, noting that they were just "doing what they were supposed to do . . . trying to please the colleges" (Cavitch 1983, p. 183).

The story raises important questions that all who accept the responsibility of educating young people must confront. Is it an educator's duty *merely* to follow the dictates of "the system," whether that system is the college board's, or the state's, or the nation's? Or do educators have a higher obligation as those who have accepted the moral responsibility to educate children? Should educators feel compelled to do more than merely follow the mandates of the system regardless of whose system it is?

In "Expelled," Cheever decried his education as having been "laced with curtseys and perfumed punctualities." He described it as an education that teaches:

> Our country is the best in the world. We are swimming in prosperity and our President is the best president in the world. We have larger apples and better cotton and faster and more beautiful machines. This makes us the greatest country in the world. (Cavitch 1983, p. 184)

Sound familiar? Is this the kind of teaching kids should expect from educators—this and lessons that drill them on a litany of facts and figures that will help them score higher on the college boards and on standardized international comparison tests so that we can show the rest of the world we are the best? Is the purpose of an education primarily to prepare students for employment and marketplace competition?

These are not insignificant questions, for as Abraham Lincoln observed (as paraphrased by Yong Zhao 2007), "The philosophy in the classroom of this generation is the philosophy of the government in the next" (p. 11). These questions go to the core of an important issue: Is it the role of schools to simply perpetuate the system we have now, or do they have a greater role to play?

You have already encountered a number of educators in these pages who believe that the responsibility of those who educate goes well beyond following the dictates of a system or merely perpetuating the status quo.

James Moffett, educator and author of the book *The Universal Schoolhouse*, believes that education should not merely mirror a society but rather correct and complement it. Neil Postman's view is similar to Lincoln's. Postman believes that education doesn't just serve a public—it creates one. Roland Barth has said, "For some reason occupants of schools seem destined to comply," and always to be determining their actions on what someone else tells them to do (2001, p. 4). But, he says, educators should recognize that they may have on occasion, an obligation of "thinking otherwise" (p. 3).

Every individual who teaches must eventually confront the question of whether her obligation rests in complying with mandates or in being willing, when the occasion calls for it, to think and act otherwise. Confronting this question isn't easy. Perhaps that is why we are warned in the Bible that not many people should presume to be teachers because those who teach will be held to a higher standard (James 3:1).

Challenging the system is risky. In *Dead Poets Society*, John Keating is fired for doing it. In Cheever's story, Laura Driscoll, his history teacher, is canned for telling her students that Sacco and Vanzetti did not deserve the treatment they received.

Still, if you read "Expelled," you will note a contrast in the way Cheever respects Laura Driscoll for teaching her students to apply their intellect to the mental and emotional state of the people of an historical period, and how he views his English teacher, Margaret Cartwright, who teaches students what they need to get into Harvard.

Well, what's wrong with educating a kid to get into Harvard? Nothing. Unless that's the only or the primary motivation for educating a student. Remember what Bill Gates told the Harvard faculty was missing in his education? It wasn't just Harvard faculty who failed to provide that missing piece of his education.

How far does the responsibility of a teacher go in determining what constitutes an education? How far must a teacher who, in her heart, truly believes that the policies and procedures of "the system" are wrong be willing to go in thinking and acting otherwise?

In the United Kingdom, a head teacher I recently read about threatened to resign unless the government scraps its plans for giving primary school children a standardized assessment test. Acknowledging that she was not against assessment, per se, she said:

> I cannot carry on seeing children doing something I don't believe in. The curriculum has been narrowed and teachers are teaching to the test. The children undergo weeks of pointless revision so they can jump through the hoops and do a 45 minute test. I cannot stand by any longer and watch this happen to the children in my school and schools across the land. (Brydon 2009, p. 26)

At the conclusion of "Expelled," it is August, and school is about to begin again. Young Cheever has no place to go; he's been expelled. He is neither sorry nor happy to put behind him an education that he says makes students "indifferent." He views his state and the situation of his prep school as symmetric—both are lost, standing on the periphery of living. What an awful fate!

The word "education" comes from the Latin verb *educare*, which means "to lead forth." Where is an education and those who provide it supposed to lead students? What is an education's destination? The answer to that question, we can be certain, is that it is meant to help students find meaning and purpose in their lives, not leave them standing on the periphery of living.

CHAPTER 14

What's So Right about Being Wrong?

*If I ran a school, I'd give the average grade to the ones who gave me all
the right answers, for being good parrots. I'd give the top grades to those
who made a lot of mistakes and told me about them, and then told me what
they learned from them.*

Buckminster Fuller

"Wrong"—such an unlovely word! Monosyllabic and absolute, it carries
with it the implication of incompetence. But should it? The truth is that being
wrong, far from being disgraceful, has a lot to offer if we are willing to accept
its gifts. Every successful scientist, inventor, entrepreneur, and artist knows
the value of making mistakes and what can be learned from them.

In fact, one of society's well-worn axioms is that we learn more from our
mistakes than we do from our successes. There is something about being
wrong that once we realize we're wrong, makes us more attentive. Albert
Einstein said, "I think and think for months and years. Ninety-nine times, the
conclusion is false. The hundredth time I am right" (www.quotes-museum
.com/quote/27468).

Yet the wisdom of this axiom is celebrated more in preaching than in practice—especially in schools. Most school practices place a high premium on
being right, and not just on being right, but upon being precisely right—the
first time. While we proclaim that school is a place where you can learn from
your mistakes, we do very little to honor mistaken effort, rewarding students
with good grades *only for giving correct answers*—the more correct answers,
the better the grade. While rewarding correct answers is as it should be, if individuals such as Albert Einstein and British philosopher/social critic Bertrand
Russell see value in being wrong, shouldn't schools?

How can we recognize worthy but mistaken effort by students in school?
Why should we bother?

Some argue that getting a poor grade on an assignment or test and being shown where you went wrong is enough acknowledgment for mistakes, that to do more would encourage the proliferation of mistakes, but that is precisely what schools should be encouraging—greater willingness on the part of students to risk being wrong. Simply deducting points for errors made and showing students where they went wrong, by itself, is hardly an incentive for young learners to learn not to fear making mistakes.

One better way is to give students an opportunity to do a test or assignment over again, correcting and eliminating their original mistakes, and then ask them what they learned from making those mistakes and from correcting them. What most students learn now from making mistakes is that they'd better not make any.

Others might object that giving students opportunities to retake tests risks encouraging lazy and irresponsible students to continue their laziness and irresponsibility when it comes to preparing for a test or assignment the first time. Granted, there is a risk, but most teachers develop excellent judgment about their students' behavior and would know when to revise their practice if they found students taking advantage of it.

Still others defer because giving students an opportunity to redo an assignment or test without some penalty raises the specter of whether we are being fair to students who got the right answer the first time.

The response to this concern depends on how you define the purpose of a test. Is it to identify areas of the lesson that students have mastered and pinpoint others that may need further teaching? Is it to certify competence? Is it to identify those who can demonstrate competence the quickest? It also depends on how you define fair: Does equal treatment always equate with fair treatment?

That is not to say that students are never given the opportunity to redo tests or assignments in school; they are in some classes, with some teachers, in some situations. These limited opportunities, though, hardly qualify for what author/educator Seymour Sarason called a "behavioral regularity" (p. 105).

We need practices that regularly acknowledge good effort that nonetheless ends in error. It is through our regular behavioral practices that we teach students what we value and how much stock they should place in what we preach. If we want to teach students to believe there is value in making mistakes and learning from them, then we must make a commitment to acknowledging genuine but flawed effort.

Fear of being wrong keeps many students from making bold efforts to think outside the conventional school paradigm of "give me the information I need, I'll give it back to you the way you gave it to me, and in return, you give me a good grade." What's worse, after years of schooling, young people often carry the fear of being wrong into their work and personal lives.

Alternatively, Alfie Kohn has shown in his book, *Punished by Rewards*, that teachers who use strategies that encourage students to focus on *what they are doing* rather than on *how well they are doing* promote high-quality, long-term involvement in learning. The strategy works well with students who have stopped trying and also with high-performing students, who tend to be more grade conscious and less prone to take risks that might threaten their grades.

> A survey of students attending an academically advanced high school found that the more they described a class as one in which the teacher emphasized understanding, improvement, trying new things, and risking mistakes (as opposed to emphasizing grades and competition), the more they liked the class, the more learning strategies they reported using, and the more they preferred challenging tasks. (Kohn 1993, p. 211)

If we want to teach students to accept the idea that a good deal of what we humans know, or think we know, is incomplete and often incorrect and that the purpose of an education is to produce people capable of recognizing error and learning from it, then we must adopt a different approach from the one that simply declares an effort right or wrong and moves on.

In *The End of Education*, Neil Postman offered a suggestion that teachers should seriously consider. Postman asked us to imagine a school organized around this principle—that "whatever ideas we have are in some sense wrong and people in schools would then proceed to learn with full consciousness of their own fallibility, as well as the fallibility of others" (1996, pp. 119–20).

That is an idea that is intellectually far more invigorating than the current paradigm in which students are taught to view information presented in textbooks and by teachers as absolute truth and seldom seriously question either. Schools organized around Postman's principle would provide a more stimulating learning environment for students and for teachers.

Young people delight in challenging the ideas of their elders and proving them wrong. A school that capitalizes on that delight would be a place worthy of students' best efforts. What student could resist a classroom that encourages the sleuth in him? What faculty would not find invigorating an intellectual setting in which they were teaching students to expose and correct error? Who doesn't love to solve a mystery?

If students came to class with the full recognition that what their textbooks or teachers or classmates or they, themselves, say might be incorrect or only partially correct, and if they were constantly encouraged to uncover what was wrong or only partially correct in what was being said or read, would that not in itself create a more reflective academic environment?

Even if students could only point out the errors or inconsistencies in what they were reading or hearing and explain why they were wrong or inconsistent but were not yet able to correct the errors and inconsistencies, wouldn't that at least be a sign of their genuine intellectual engagement—a first step along the path to wisdom?

Teachers could surrender their role as information merchants in favor of a role of guiding students to be effective analyzers and error detectors. Creative teachers, like other creative people, would thrive on a challenge like this.

If students got used to carefully examining what they were reading and being taught, and probing for errors, inconsistencies, and even prejudices, that alone would show them there is no disgrace in being wrong. For when they understood that everyone makes mistakes, even those whose teaching they admire, they would see less disgrace in risking being wrong themselves.

We need school practices that teach students there is no disgrace in honest effort that turns out to be wrong—practices that teach that being wrong, when approached with the right attitude, spurs human beings on to greater understanding and achievement.

Once young people discover that the path to knowledge cannot bypass but must travel through the landscape of error, they will not be so terrified of being wrong. What would be wrong with that?

CHAPTER 15

What's So Right about Being Wrong?—An Example

I was leading a high school class through an analysis of Robert Frost's poem "The Road Not Taken." We had established the fact that the poem was describing choices we make in life, the little ones and the big ones. I made sure that students paid close attention to the fact that the roads in question had diverged in a "yellow wood," and we discussed the significance of that. We spent some time looking at the lines:

> I shall be telling this with a sigh
> Somewhere ages and ages hence:
> Two roads diverged in a wood, and I—
> I took the one less traveled by,
> And that has made all the difference.
> (www.poemhunter.com/poem/the-road-not-taken/The Road Not Taken)

After some discussion of the various possible meanings of the words "sigh" and "difference," I asked students if they thought the poet was satisfied with the road he had chosen.

When there was no response, I suggested that perhaps he wasn't satisfied with his choice, since he called his poem "The Road Not Taken" rather than "The Road I Took." I asked students to look back through the poem and see if they could find evidence to support my hypothesis. A few minutes passed in silence. Finally a student raised his hand.

"I don't think you are right about that, Mr. Connolly."

"Really! Why not, Brian?"

"Well, if you look carefully at the time sequence of the poem, you realize that there is no way for the poet to know whether the choice he made was a good one or a bad one."

Brian proceeded to point out that the poem described a choice that had just been made. True, he continued, the poet knew his choice was a significant one, but whether or not he'd ultimately be satisfied with that choice, he could not yet know. As for why Frost called his poem "The Road *Not* Taken," Brian said that it's human nature to wonder, "What would have happened if I'd taken that other path?"

As the so-called expert in that class, I could have been embarrassed by Brian's perceptiveness. After all, I was the teacher and an American literature major. But I was thrilled.

Brian had internalized a lesson that I'd taught earlier in the year using Hemingway's *The Old Man and the Sea*—that an intelligent person doesn't just accept ideas, information, beliefs, or even "proven" facts. He walks around them and into them; he questions them and confronts them. In this way, he strives to establish if they are wise or not, accurate or not, truthful or not. Isn't that what we expect educated people to do?

In *The Old Man and the Sea*, Hemingway told the story of how an old man teaches his young protégé that the long-held wisdom of the village elders could be wrong. Santiago, the old fisherman, sails out well beyond the boundaries, where all the other men of the village are convinced it is unsafe to go.

Although he is not able to bring back his large catch in one piece, he has nonetheless successfully challenged the conviction of his fellow fishermen and shown them they were wrong. His reward is that he can now lie down and dream of lions, knowing that he'd been fearless enough to go beyond the boundaries of conventional wisdom and to establish a new truth.

> Each generation that discovers something from its experience must pass that on, but it must pass that on with a delicate balance of respect and disrespect, so that the race (now that it is aware of the disease to which it is liable) does not inflict its errors too rigidly on its youth, but it does pass on the accumulated wisdom, plus the wisdom that it may not be wisdom. (Feynman 1999, p. 188)

The disease to which Noble Prize–winning physicist Richard Feynman refers is the idea that what "experts" say must be unquestionably right. Can you think of a better role for a teacher than to teach students to be confident in their ability to sift through the accumulated wisdom of the generations and determine what is wisdom and what is not?

CHAPTER 16

Learning to Love Their *Questions*

Young children are notorious lovers of questions and sometimes drive parents to desperation with an endless array of them. "Please, Katy, let Mommy rest and save the questions for later." So why do children ask fewer and fewer questions as they proceed through their school years?

Are we doing something wrong—something that snuffs out rather than inspires student questions and the natural curiosity that arouses them? Are there things that we can do in the classroom to help students reclaim their natural inquisitiveness?

Research on classroom questioning practices says yes to both questions. The fact that well-intentioned teachers utilize classroom practice they themselves were subjected to during their school days is a direct cause of students asking fewer and fewer questions in their classes.

The good news is that most students' natural curiosity is not dead; it is merely anesthetized by poor practice, which can be reversed by teachers who value students' questions and who structure their classes so that students are encouraged to ask them. The cure is simple, but not easy.

The first prerequisite for curing an illness is to acknowledge it. No problem there. Virtually everyone is aware of the lack of curiosity many students bring to the classroom. The next stage—the cure—involves treating the underlying causes of the disorder. This gets a bit more complicated. So let's take a look at what stifles the natural inquisitiveness of young people when they are in school.

In *Revisiting "The Culture of the School and the Problem of Change"* Seymour Sarason provided the following data about question-asking behavior in classrooms:

1. Across the different studies the range of rate of teacher questions per half hour is from 45–150.

2. When asked, educators as well as other groups vastly underestimate the rate of teacher questions, the estimated range being 12–20 per half hour.
3. From 67 to 95 percent of all teacher questions require "straight recall" from the student.
4. Children ask fewer than two questions per half hour.
5. The greater the tendency for a teacher to ask straight recall questions, the fewer the questions initiated by children.
6. The more a teacher asks "personally relevant" questions, the higher the rate of questioning on the part of children.
7. The rate of questions by children does not seem to vary with IQ level or with social-class background. (1996, pp. 105–6)

Teachers and administrators who read Sarason's research are surprised by the number of questions teachers ask during a thirty-minute period. But when they examine the data more closely, their initial surprise dissipates. If 67 to 95 percent of the questions a teacher asks are recall questions, it is easy to see how she could ask that many in a thirty-minute period, particularly when students ask so few during that same period of time. To remedy this problem, we need to look at points 5 and 6.

Point 6 tells us that the more "personally relevant" the questions a teacher asks, the higher the rate of questions the students ask. Point 5 indicates that the greater the tendency of the teacher to ask "straight recall" questions, the fewer questions students ask.

A steady dose of strictly recall questions makes it clear to students that it isn't their questions that matter—it is the teacher's or the textbook's questions and students' ability to answer them that matter. This is a situation, though, that can be reversed in classrooms by teachers who have the commitment, the nerve, and the patience to do it.

What teachers need to do is open up their lessons for more student questions and then allow students to grapple with their questions until they find answers to them. This sounds easier than it actually is. Let's take a look at why.

Those classroom questioning regularities noted by Sarason are the result of training most teachers receive and the impressions they develop over time about what is expected of them, impressions reinforced by administrators, parents, and even the students themselves. In *The Courage to Teach: Exploring the Inner Landscape of a Teacher's Life*, Parker Palmer described what most teachers experience when they enter a classroom:

> Like most professionals, I was taught to occupy space, not open it: after all, we are the ones who know, so we have an obligation to tell others about it! Even

though I have rejected that nonsensical norm, I still feel guilty when I defy it. A not-so-small voice within me insists that if I am not filling all the available space with my own knowledge, I am not earning my keep. (1998, p. 132)

There's that awful word "defy" again. Yet a certain amount of defiance is what a teacher who cares about children must cultivate to overcome the kinds of classroom behavior that work against students becoming engaged and independent learners.

Exacerbating the problem that Palmer described are increasingly more prescriptive curriculums and an increased reliance on high-stakes standardized tests. Those who promote such curriculums and tests often assert that they are merely meant to be guides. But as Sarason pointed out, teachers reply, "What they want to know at the end of the year, and what I will be judged by, are the achievement test scores of my children" (1996, p. 109).

And yet, defying this fossilized classroom questioning paradigm can be done successfully despite the obstacles. Remember Sandra Hahn and Karen Rayle? There is much to be gained from this particular defiance.

To teach students to love learning rather than simply endure it, we must teach them to love questions—their own as well as others. We can do this by encouraging (even requiring) their questions, as Karen Rayle does. When individuals stop asking questions, they cease being curious, and when they cease being curious, they are no longer learning. One might even suggest, as Einstein did, they are no longer truly living, merely existing: "He who can no longer pause to wonder and stand rapt in awe, is as good as dead; his eyes are closed" (www.brainyquote.com/quotes/keywords/pause.html). That is why encouraging students to ask questions and to pursue answers to their questions is critical to teaching them to love learning.

Still, even when we defy our own professional training and open up the classroom space for student questions, the battle will not be completely won. There are still more expectations we must be prepared to challenge—those of the students.

In *Letters to a Young Poet*, Ranier Maria Rilke responded to the questions an aspiring young poet sent him by advising the man to "be patient . . . and try to love the questions." It's excellent advice for students, as well as for an aspiring poet, but it's not advice that is easy to take. Notice Rilke's use of the word "try."

Learning to love questions and to live with the uncertainty that prompts them is tough; students are taught to love answers and to love getting them quickly—from their teachers, their textbooks, and now the Internet. Just as teachers have been taught that the classroom is where *they* must fill up the space, students have been taught the classroom is where *they* should expect to get answers.

Rilke's young poet didn't write to him hoping for the kind of answer that Rilke sent him. He wrote wanting Rilke to give him a master's answer to the question "Are my poems good enough to be published?" He was impatient; he wanted to be told the answer, not have to spend time on his own searching for it.

I do not know how the young poet responded to Rilke's advice. I do know from my personal experience as a learner and as a teacher that when students learn to love and respect questions, their own as well as those of others, and believe in their ability to find answers to them, they learn to love learning.

Under the guidance of caring teachers who encourage and value their questions, young learners can rediscover the joy of asking questions and of finding answers to them. "So, Katy, the class and I are waiting for your questions."

STRATEGIES FOR GETTING STUDENTS TO ASK THEIR QUESTIONS

1. From the first day of school, encourage students to ask question that interest them about a subject and each unit of study.
2. Be prepared for the fact that in the beginning, students will mimic the kinds of simple questions teachers or textbooks have traditionally asked. You can teach them to ask higher-order thinking questions by constructing open-ended questions that don't have a simple factual recall answer and by asking questions that require divergent thinking.
3. Don't judge student questions, but encourage them to ask questions that personally interest them.
4. Before beginning a unit, conduct a class brainstorming activity in which you encourage students to formulate the kinds of questions they would like to find answers to. Join them in this activity by adding questions that personally interest you.
5. Model question-asking by thinking aloud about questions that occur to you as you move through a unit. Make these questions ones that don't have a straight recall answer.
6. Use exit cards — 3 x 5 cards on which students can write questions that occurred to them during a lesson. Invite them to put these questions in a box as they exit. This activity is particularly good for soliciting questions from quieter members of the class. No names on the cards, please.

CHAPTER 17

Teaching Students to Value Commitment

In the movie *The Karate Kid*, Daniel Larusso, a lonely adolescent, moves with his mom from New Jersey to, for him, a less welcoming environment in Los Angeles. Fortunately, Daniel develops a friendship with a Japanese handyman who works in his apartment complex.

Daniel's school experience is miserable; he is being harassed by a group of young toughs, all of them members of the same karate dojo. When he discovers that his new friend and soon-to-be mentor, Mr. Miyagi, has mastered karate, Daniel begs Miyagi to teach him. At first Miyagi refuses, telling Daniel that karate is a discipline, not a weapon for beating people up.

When Miyagi discovers that the local dojo sensei approves of and even encourages his boys to use their karate skills to physically harass Daniel, he agrees to teach Daniel karate—on the condition that Daniel consent to enter a karate tournament in which his tormentors will also be participants.

Daniel's initiation into karate training and what he learns from it can be instructive for teachers, who should design lessons that show students the value of commitment. As they are about to begin the training, Miyagi asks Daniel if he is ready, and Daniel responds, "Yeah, I guess so." Miyagi immediately confronts his pupil's cavalier approach to the upcoming learning challenge:

> Daniel-san, must talk. Walk on road, hm? Walk left side, safe. Walk right side, safe. Walk middle, sooner or later [makes squish gesture] get squish just like grape. Here, karate, same thing. Either you karate do "yes" or karate do "no." You karate do "guess so" [makes squish gesture], just like grape. Understand?

Miyagi is pointing out to his pupil that without genuine commitment to what he is about to learn, there will be no real learning. Daniel must either wholeheartedly commit to the learning experience, or he would be better off not even to undertake it. A cavalier "Yeah, I guess so" will not get the job done. This is a lesson that all students must learn sooner or later regardless of what they are trying to learn—and, of course, the sooner the better.

Teachers who aim to teach students anything, let alone to love learning, must begin by teaching them the importance of commitment. That is not an easy task, particularly with students who may be disaffected or simply nonchalant, like Daniel. A teacher must give some thought to how she will teach her students the importance of commitment. She should never assume students already have learned the value of it. Notice how Miyagi teaches Daniel this critical first lesson not simply by lecturing about it but by creating an actual experience in which Daniel will learn the importance of commitment.

Handing Daniel a headband to seal their teacher/pupil compact, Miyagi declares the basic terms of every successful teacher/pupil partnership: "I agree to teach; you agree to learn; I say, you do. Understand?" Daniel says he does, but Miyagi knows and events will prove he doesn't. How often do most students give any serious thought to their responsibilities in the teacher/ learner partnership?

Once the training begins, we get a picture of how a skillful teacher uses drill and practice to secure more than mere surface learning from it.

It would be easy to mistake the regimen of training that Miyagi puts Daniel through as just drill and practice exercises that teach karate techniques. To do so would be to miss a major objective of those exercises, which is to establish the commitment that Miyagi has demanded of Daniel. At this point, it is as important that Daniel learn what commitment will require of him as it is for him to learn karate moves. Delving right into the subject matter before students truly understand the commitment they must make to master it is a mistake teachers sometimes make.

Once the training is under way, Miyagi has Daniel wash and polish a lot full of cars, sand a sun deck, paint a backyard fence, and finally, paint his (Miyagi's) house. Frustrated and angry, and seeing little connection between what he is being asked to do and karate, Daniel rebels. Think of your own students' acts of rebellion.

Miyagi returns from fishing. Daniel confronts him when Miyagi tells him he has learned plenty from all the chores he's done:

> Daniel: I've learned plenty! I've learned how to sand your decks maybe! How about wash your cars, paint your house, paint your fence. I've learned plenty! [Have you ever had a student question the value of what you asked him to do?]
> Miyagi: Oh, Daniel-san, not everything is as seems.
> Daniel: Oh bullshit! I'm going home man!

Then comes a moment that leads to Daniel's recognition of what commitment to what he has been asked to do eventually will produce. Miyagi demonstrates how all of those tasks he has made Daniel do have taught him the karate skills he wants to learn.

The expression on Daniel's face tells us all we need to know. It indicates that he now does understand what fulfilling his part of the teacher/student compact can produce. He now recognizes the value of all those "boring" tasks that he has been doing. From this point on, he can accept what his teacher will require of him. He's committed both to the work ahead and to trusting his teacher.

There are a number of lessons a teacher can learn from a master teacher like Miyagi. First, she can learn about the importance of teaching students to trust their teacher. Trust, as we know, is essential in the pupil/teacher relationship. A teacher should not merely assume she will have it or even earn it over time by simply doing what she normally does. It is not as easy to establish as we would wish it to be—especially when we are asking someone to do something they aren't particularly inclined to do. Mr. Miyagi understood that. So does Reno Taini. That's why he begins a school year with his Chair of Respect activity.

In an essay, "On Obstinacy in Belief," from *The World's Last Night and Other Essays*, C. S. Lewis talked about how essential this issue of trust is in situations where one individual seeks to help another:

> In getting a dog out of a trap, in extracting a thorn from a child's finger, in teaching a boy to swim or trying to rescue one who can't, in getting a frightened beginner over a nasty place on the mountain, the one fatal obstacle may be their distrust. . . . We ask them to believe that what is painful will relieve their pain, and that which looks dangerous is their only safety. We ask them to accept apparent impossibilities: that moving the paw farther back into the trap is the only way to get it out—that hurting the finger very much more will stop the finger from hurting, that water which is obviously permeable will resist and support the body . . . that to go higher and onto an exposed ledge is the way not to fall. (1987, p. 23)

When a teacher structures a lesson that shows students what genuine commitment can produce, a student's trust in that teacher increases. The trust I am talking about is the trust a student develops when after having rewritten an essay three or four times at the teacher's insistence, he finally comes away with an A and knows that what he has written is good.

It's the kind of trust a student develops when after weeks of being required to explain *why* she worked out her homework math problems the way she did, she is able to complete a challenging problem she never thought she could solve.

It's the kind of trust a student develops for a science, history, literature, or math teacher when the student starts to appreciate history, science, literature, or math in the way historians, scientists, mathematicians, or writers appreciate those subjects.

Confrontation can be an effective tool for building students' commitment to learning and trust in their teacher. If you have never seen *The Karate Kid*, or if you have watched it but not paid careful attention to Miyagi's teaching approach, rent the movie and watch the scenes I've just described. One of the things you will notice is that the confrontation scene is no accident. Miyagi has planned for it. In fact, he structured his lesson to produce it. The day of the confrontation is the only day he leaves Daniel alone all day while he goes off fishing. Just a coincidence? Of course not.

Confrontation—the right kind of confrontation that is under control and initiated with love, and has been thought through and even planned for in advance—is not an impediment to learning but can be a facilitator of it. I'm certain that Mrs. Martin anticipated a confrontation with a student like Robert once report cards came out. While I may have been surprised by how well she handled it, I'm sure she wasn't. She had prepared for it.

It is too easy for students to sleepwalk through learning experiences and miss the benefit of them. They often need a wake-up call in order to fully appreciate the value of commitment in a learning experience. Lecturing about the importance of commitment and about students fulfilling their part in the pupil/teacher pact will never be as effective as providing an experience in which they discover firsthand its importance—and rewards.

To be sure, the wake-up call must be given with love, but it can be confrontational. Mrs. Martin understood that. Recall how Robert reacted after he got one. Mr. Miyagi understood it too. Watch the movie, and note the way Daniel approaches his learning tasks and his teacher after the scene I've described.

Commitment to learning sounds like a jail sentence to students who have yet to learn the value of it. A good teacher takes time to teach students that, as in any relationship they hope will develop into love, this one too demands that they must make a commitment to it. And when they do . . .

Well, anyone who has ever fallen in love should be able to finish that sentence.

CHAPTER 18

Revising Our Reductionist View of Teaching and Learning

School does not have in its institutional mind that teachers have a creative role: it sees them as technicians doing a technical job, and for this the word training [teacher training] is perfectly appropriate.

Seymour Papert, in *The Children's Machine*, p. 70

A major reason why the teaching profession fails to get the respect it deserves is that many people, even some educators, fail to understand the complexity of the teaching and learning processes. They wrongly view teaching as a series of technical activities and teachers as technicians whose job it is to produce "educated" students in much the same way that GE, for instance, produces washing machines or microwave ovens.

That is why many who try to reform the schoolhouse spend so much time talking about re-engineering—the curriculum, the schedule, the length of the school day or school year, the time spent on subjects like science and math, and the teaching practices teachers use. It is why they establish control strategies such as teacher-proof instructional materials, mandated curriculums, standardized tests, and accountability policies that attempt to force teachers and students to do things the way they recommend they be done.

When these strategies fail to produce the results they want, policymakers who push these re-engineering efforts resort to punishing students, their teachers, and schools for not making adequate yearly progress.

What many policymakers need to do is to *re-form* their own view of teachers and students. Teachers should not be viewed as technicians, nor students as simply raw material to be fashioned into the kinds of workers the marketplace demands.

That view demeans teachers and students and the learning process as well. It is the main reason why many schools continue to look and operate like factories, where students receive a conveyor-belt education, moving from one classroom to another to have some math inserted here, some science there, some social studies a little further on, and so on down the line. It explains why more voices are heard declaring that one day, information technologies will replace teachers in the classroom. After all, we've managed to replace production workers with machines. Why can't we accomplish the same thing in our schools?

The failure of policymakers, the general public, the press, and even many educators to recognize the complexity of teaching has been documented by a number of people who have taken the time to look closely at what effective teaching requires. In addition to Seymour Papert, there is Dr. William Glasser, author of *The Quality School: Managing Students Without Coercion.*

> Almost everyone in our society shares a huge misconception about teaching. By "everyone" I mean not only the general public, but also teachers as well as parents, administrators, school board members, politicians, educational news reporters, and even the college professors who run teacher-preparation programs. What almost all fail to understand is that being an effective teacher may be the most difficult job of all in our society. (1990, p. 14)

Teachers are not technicians, nor are students technical challenges to be worked on like fixing a toaster. Both should be viewed more like artists whose work is to create and re-create.

Think for a moment about what an effective teacher must do in a classroom: construct engaging lessons and assignments; empathize with a variety of students; orchestrate a mixture of classroom learning activities, not just for students as individuals, but also for students in groups; try to figure out what is going through the minds of students when they are uncooperative or uncommunicative; and envision what each student can be when he is at his best.

Additionally, both the teacher and her students must re-create in their own minds the knowledge base created by others whose work they are studying—and when they are really on their game as creative artists, add to that knowledge. We readily accept the notion that someone who is gazing with appreciation at Vermeer's painting "The Milkmaid" is, in a sense, re-creating the scene in the painting in his mind and even adding to it. Yet we have trouble ascribing the same artistry to someone who is studying the Pythagorean Theorem in a geometry class.

If we want bright, creative people teaching children and if we want children to be bright and creative, how we choose to view them will determine how we treat them. How we treat them will determine the results we get.

How many bright, creative people will we attract to a job that is considered technical, repetitive, and uncreative—one that anyone can do if we only give him the right protocols, and in fact, even a computer can do it if we program it correctly? How many students find inspiring the idea that the function of a school and their teachers is to manufacture them into a form that is desirable for consumption in the marketplace?

The most distressing part of the Papert observation is that educators—teachers, administrators, and those running teacher-preparation programs and staff development workshops—too easily buy into that kind of thinking, as evidenced in this quote from Neil Postman.

> Many [educators] have focused their attention on the engineering of learning, their journals being filled with accounts of research that show this way or that to be better for teaching reading, mathematics, or social studies. The evidence for the superiority of one method over another is usually given in the language of statistics, which, in spite of its abstract nature, is strangely referred to as "hard evidence." This gives the profession a sense of making progress, and sometimes delusions of grandeur. (1996, p. 26)

When educators adopt the belief that they have been trained in the best method to teach a subject or concept and simply follow that method instead of using their own intuition, imagination, and common sense in teaching, they reduce themselves to being technicians. Technicians seldom question the techniques they have been trained to use or the principles behind them. They are not expected to; they are expected to simply apply them.

The truth is that effective teaching involves much more than simply utilizing a series of teaching techniques we've been taught. In fact, the best definition I've come across for teaching is a definition that the *Boston Globe* sportswriter Bob Ryan used to describe NBA officiating. If I may borrow Mr. Ryan's definition and apply it to teaching, then teaching would be defined as "an art embellished with common sense."

Those who truly love learning and want to help students love it too must start with a different view of teaching and learning than the reductionist one that is so dominant today. They must begin with the conviction that teaching is an art that demands teachers be intelligent, intuitive, creative, learning strategists, and willing to experiment with new tools and methods, including ones they invent themselves. While they always remain open to learning new teaching approaches, they don't feel compelled to rely on methods that someone else has told them are the best, if not the only, way to teach effectively.

We must have teachers who approach what they do in the same way that artists approach what they do—in other words, with a willingness to listen to the voice coming from within telling them not to fear experimenting, even if it means breaking the "established" protocols to get better results.

If teachers want to teach students to love learning, they must be teachers who refuse to treat students as if they are consumer goods they are engineering for university or the marketplace. They must believe, and show students they believe, that students are also creative artists whose task it is not simply to uncritically absorb established knowledge but to learn to critically analyze it and use it to create new knowledge.

Once those who teach take seriously the idea that teachers aren't technicians and learners aren't engineering problems, then they can work to bring other Americans over to a more realistic view of education. The responsibility of educators, as Postman and others have pointed out, isn't just "to serve a public," it is "to create one" (1996, p. 18). That responsibility includes creating a public that understands and appreciates the complexity of both teaching and learning.

CHAPTER 19

We Don't Just Love You, We Need You

Our youth now love luxury. They have bad manners, contempt for authority; they show disrespect for their elders and love chatter in place of exercise; they no longer rise when elders enter the room; they contradict their parents, chatter before company; gobble up their food and tyrannize their teachers.

Socrates

There is a tendency among those in the older generation to look down upon the young and to wonder if they will ever measure up to the standards that we, their elders, have established. Many of us, conveniently forgetting our own youth and how adults viewed us during those years, strongly suspect they will not. Youth today, many of us believe, just don't have the character or intellectual depth to persevere in, let alone improve, the civilization their forebearers labored so long and so hard to build.

This pessimistic view—which Professor John Gardner labeled the "drying reservoir" conviction (1995, p. 126)—has, as the quote from Socrates attests, been with us for some time. It is as dismissive of young people in our day as it was when Socrates first uttered it.

Certainly, there are some youngsters today, as there are in every age, for whom Socrates' claim is very accurate. Then the same description could easily have been applied to some adults in his day and can just as easily be applied to some in ours. However, as a blanket statement about youth (or adults), such a claim is a blatant exaggeration.

The bracing but seldom-acknowledged truth is that the young are capable of great accomplishments and contributions to society and civilization. The fact that they are rarely asked to or expected to accounts for why they don't.

Indeed, much of what we adults do to young people before they reach adulthood amounts to putting a bit in their mouths and a bridle around their necks and announcing to them: "You're not ready to be responsible yet, so sit down and eat your spinach and keep quiet until we can educate you to be as sensible, intelligent, reliable, trustworthy, and creative as we are." No wonder many young people chafe at the "education" we try to give them.

If we love our children, we will give them a different message:

> We need you and your skills and talents. No, not when you graduate high school or university, but right now. Our nation and our world need what you have to offer. What's more, we need you to develop your skills and talents to the highest level of excellence now and throughout your lifetime.
>
> We are facing some very challenging problems today: genocides, AIDS, infant deaths, global warming, extreme hunger in some areas, national conflicts that seem to defy peaceful solutions, and crime and deteriorating living conditions in many cities. We need to find solutions to these problems and others, and we simply will not be able to do it without you. We need you!

"To be needed," wrote John Gardner in *Excellence: Can We Be Equal and Excellent Too?*, "is one of the richest forms of moral and spiritual nourishment; and not to be needed is one of the most severe forms of psychic deprivation" (1961, pp. 152–53). He goes on to say that any society that allows its young to feel useless is not simply neglecting them but also depriving them of a powerful spiritual tonic.

John F. Kennedy knew this. That's why young people responded to him when he challenged them in his inaugural speech—"Ask not what your country can do for you; ask what you can do for your country"—and why they came forward en masse to volunteer when he established the Peace Corps.

Educators owe it to the young people they teach to call them to action to do important work both inside and outside of the schoolhouse. In every case where I have done this or seen other people do it, I've seen students' enthusiasm rise to the challenge like a huge ocean swell—a tsunami of positive response. Nonetheless, adults as a whole tend to vastly underestimate the desire and the potential of young people to make contributions to our society while they are in school.

In 1990 during the first Persian Gulf War, students at Varnum Brook Middle School, with the encouragement of one of their teachers, were writing letters and sending packages to service personnel stationed in Saudi Arabia. One of those units was Observation Squadron 2. When its commander, Lt. Colonel Clifford M. Acree, became a POW, the students were suddenly cast into the national spotlight.

The colonel had written the students thanking them for their contributions to his squadron. Now he was a prisoner of war. The national media got hold of the story that first appeared in the town newspaper.

Three Boston TV stations, plus NBC *Nightly News* and *Inside Edition*, as well as state and national newspapers, appeared at the school, all wanting to do stories about students who were concerned with what was happening in the world and who were trying to make a contribution to the lives of others. Many reporters expressed surprise at the intelligence, articulateness, and commitment of the students they interviewed. One reporter told me, "It is a pleasure to talk with kids who know what is going on, who can express themselves articulately, and who care about someone other than themselves."

Frankly, my staff and I were surprised by the media's surprise. Service to others was the norm rather than the exception among our students. It was one of our school's core values.

The year before the Gulf War, students had been making books for children living in shelters for the homeless. Other students, with their faculty advisor, had formed a group called Kids Who Care, and each month they visited shut-ins at a local nursing home. The sixth graders hosted senior citizens at an annual Sixth Grade/Senior Citizens Spelling Bee, and the school's band and chorus gave concerts at the senior citizens hall. Seventh graders conducted a campaign to heighten awareness about the importance of rainforests and raised money to send to groups who were trying to protect those valuable resources.

The same year students were writing to soldiers, others were involved in a program for reading to and tutoring younger students, and, as they had for so many years in the past, students were donating large amounts of food products to local needy families at Thanksgiving and Christmas.

Many schools have mission statements stating that one of the goals of their education is to empower students to make positive contributions to their community, their nation, and the world—not just in the future, when they become adults, but while they are young and in school. Young people welcome this kind of challenge and respond to it.

The reason why adults are so often surprised by young people's ability to make a remarkable difference in our world is because those adults have fallen victim to Socrates' damning assessment of young people (even wise people say foolish things at times), and so they don't ask or expect young people to make significant contributions.

Those who love children and want to give them the kind of education that will empower them and make their lives meaningful and purposeful must eschew Socrates' unwise assessment and the "drying reservoir" conviction. When working with children, they must always keep in mind and act upon

Gardner's reminder that to be needed is one of the richest forms of moral and spiritual nourishment, and not to be needed is one of the severest forms of psychic deprivation.

Young people know this. Educators who love their students recognize it too and make certain that the youngsters they teach understand that they are not only loved but needed.

CHAPTER 20

Learning to Love Unlearning

The illiterate of the future are not those that cannot read or write. They are those that cannot learn, unlearn, and relearn.

Alvin Toffler

Learning will be a joyful experience if it is approached with the right attitude and if the learning experience itself is structured in a way that provokes curiosity, wonder, and surprise. There is one aspect of learning, though, that isn't much fun for most people even when it produces, or maybe especially when it produces, surprise and astonishment. I'm talking about unlearning—that part of learning that we must train ourselves to love because it is often particularly painful, awkward, and frustrating but nonetheless, essential.

When my wife and I moved to Thailand for our first international teaching experience, I quickly learned that I'd have to unlearn some things I had learned in the United States and had always taken for granted. Driving provided a prime example.

In the United States, the business side of the car is on the left, but in Thailand and other countries, it is on the right. So for several weeks, I found myself instinctively slipping into the passenger seat of my Toyota before realizing that if I wanted to go anywhere, I'd have to slide over to the driver's seat on the right-hand side. Then, since the driver's instruments are also reversed, I often found myself signaling turns with my windshield wipers and using my directionals to try to switch on my headlights.

Thais are used to such *farlong* (foreigner) mistakes and pay little attention to them. Even so, I felt chagrined by my ineptitude and tried to disguise it by rummaging through the glove compartment, pretending I intended to get in on the passenger side all along. My chagrin quickly changed to fear when my driving mistakes began to be life threatening.

In the United States, a driver flashes her headlights to invite you to pull out ahead of her at an intersection. Her flashing lights tell you she intends to slow down or stop and let you go first. Not so in Thailand. That same signal means that an oncoming driver has no intention of slowing down, so you'd better stay where you are until she's passed.

After narrowly avoiding several potentially fatal collisions, I finally realized what Thai drivers meant when they flashed their headlights. With that realization came the recognition that what I'd learned in one situation may be useless and even dangerous in another. I'd have to unlearn it—and quickly.

It's ironic that we must sometimes abandon formerly useful learning in order to learn something new. That irony becomes poignant when it is an educator who must abandon previously mastered practice in order to be more effective. One can almost see the fates snickering into their fists like juveniles who have hidden a brick behind a beach ball and are waiting for an unwary bather to come by and kick it.

Nonetheless, distressing as it may be, we must face the reality that in order to prepare students to be successful as twenty-first-century citizens, we must be ready to relinquish a number of our most enduring beliefs about teaching and learning and the practices we've built upon those beliefs.

Change requires letting go of old ideas and welcoming new ones. We know that, but knowing it doesn't make the doing easier. Remember as a child how it felt when your dad took the training wheels off your bicycle and you had to learn how to ride without them? It is only the promise of something better, some unparalleled achievement, that makes the discomfort worthwhile. With that in mind, let's review some of the unlearning educators have already accomplished over the years before going on to what yet remains to be unlearned.

Remember when virtually everyone, including educators, was convinced that intelligence was a fixed immutable gift of heredity? Remember when we believed that all students learn the same way, even though some of us had vague intuitions about learning styles?

Can you recall when schools tracked students into college, business, technical, and general tracks, or when students of color were separated from white students, or when students with disabilities were segregated into separate classrooms because people believed they couldn't be educated with the "regular" kids? We learned to unlearn all of that previous learning. Still, there is more to be unlearned, and now I turn to that.

OVERRELIANCE ON TEXTBOOKS

Textbooks are written by committees for publishers who want to sell their books in the biggest markets. These publishers and their textbook-writing committees work assiduously to avoid putting anything in the text that might be controversial. Anyone who has read textbooks in science or history, or any other subject for that matter, would have to admit that reading them was like swallowing dust; they are that dry. Textbooks lack an author's voice. Most are no more stimulating than an office memo.

There are other problems as well. Textbooks come across as if they are the last word, the gospel on whatever they are covering, and more often than not, they lead teachers astray into bad teaching. Remember John Keating in *Dead Poet's Society*? There was a good reason he had his students tear out the introductory pages of their English literature anthology. Those pages contained a lot of bad advice about how to read poetry.

Among the most important skills students need to develop to be successful as human beings are critical judgment, empathy, and sensitivity. Our humanity and our very existence depend on such things. So where do textbooks—which present a subject in a series of packets of established truths—teach critical judgment? Where is the textbook that presents history in such a way that students can empathize with real people in any era? Where is the science textbook that presents science as a struggle to understand instead of a finished product of experiments, axioms, and natural laws?

If students are to learn to appreciate science and scientists for what they are, they need to read books by science writers such as Carl Sagan, Stephen Jay Gould, James Gleick, Richard Feynman, and others.

If students are to understand history, they should have an opportunity to experience how historians such as Barbara Tuchman, David Halberstam, Richard Brookhiser, Catherine Drinker Bowen, and Howard Zinn present a period or personality from the past.

In composition classes, books by William Zinsser, Natalie Goldberg, and Julia Cameron would be more instructive than a textbook.

In economics, the work of E. F. Schumacher, John Kenneth Galbraith, John Maynard Keynes, and Mohandas Gandhi (yes, Gandhi) should be the focus of reading rather than a textbook, whose primary function should be as a supplement rather than the main course.

TRUST THE EXPERTS

Remember Richard Feynman's counsel that educators must learn and teach students that it is acceptable, and even expedient, to doubt the experts (chapter

15)? This advice seems counterintuitive, even crazy, doesn't it? After all, we who teach are supposed to learn and pass on the accumulated wisdom of our race to the younger members of it, aren't we? Isn't that why we have schools and school-teachers? Isn't that what society has a right to expect of us? Well, yes and no.

We do have an obligation to pass on the accumulated wisdom of our race, but we have an equal obligation to cultivate in ourselves and pass on to our young people the conviction that we and they may have to test the veracity of that wisdom. The responsibility to test the reliability of accumulated wisdom is what we refer to as critical thinking.

We don't spend a lot of time examining mistaken ideas from the past in schools, but we should.

A list of the more grievous errors from the past and present could fill a library. It would include such tenaciously held convictions as the world is flat, Earth is the center of the universe, man was not meant to fly, the universe runs like a well-designed machine, the Chinese Communists will take over Vietnam, the market will correct itself without government intervention, and computers are "smarter" than people.

The list could go on and on, but the point is that human beings, even "experts," are prone to error. Add the fact that human life changes when things are added to it (new technologies) or subtracted from it (strongly held superstitions) and you understand that all of us have to be ready to unlearn what we have previously learned or simply believed.

Blind acceptance of the wisdom of experts, regardless of whatever field those experts come from or however many letters follow their names, is the antithesis of wisdom. Even experts know that. Feynman is, one should remember, a Noble Prize–winning physicist—an "expert" in his field.

Educators must learn to question the experts and teach students to do likewise. That doesn't mean to dismiss the experts or disrespect what they have to say. Doubt and dismissal are not the same thing, and those who doubt often have more respect for what they choose to question than those who blindly accept it.

Look again at Feynman's advice. He tells us we must pass on the wisdom of a generation, along with the wisdom that it may not be wisdom. In other words, we must exercise critical judgment and help those we teach to exercise theirs.

There are many ways to teach students how to develop their ability to critically judge what they hear and read and see. One of the best ways is to demonstrate our own ability to do it. This is not the place to go the many other ways to do it. I have included in a textbox one suggestion made by educator Neil Postman.

There is wisdom in utilizing the wisdom of experts. The problem lies in blindly following it without considering the value or validity of it. The latter habit is what we and our students need to unlearn.

CONFIDENCE IN THE VALUE OF GRADES

So many people have written about the foolhardiness of using numbers and letters to assess student performance that it feels redundant and is, to visit this topic again. Yet asking teachers and the general public to surrender their conviction about grades is like asking the people in the thirteenth century to surrender their conviction that the world is flat—some are willing, most are not.

It's not hard to fathom why it is so difficult to give up an idea that has been with us for so long that it has come to be a cherished conviction. Surrendering a long-standing belief, even an erroneous one that has served as a foundational piece of our educational structure for so long, makes the ground shiver and feel unsteady beneath us. We fear for the safety of the whole structure.

When you add to that the fact that we live in an age that believes you can quantify everything and to do less is to capitulate to whims of personal bias (conveniently forgetting that number and letter grades have biases too), then to even imagine giving up grading seems to be asking too much of us.

But surrender our conviction about the value of numerical and letter grades we must. Grades undermine students' motivation to learn by keeping their focus (and often their parents' focus) on the grade rather than on the learning. Numerical and letter grades encourage another bad habit. This one has to do with teachers and other test designers.

William Glasser has pointed out that it is much easier for teachers to test or evaluate whether students can remember something than it is for them to figure out how to evaluate whether students can use the information they've learned (1990, p. 66). The result is we have a profusion of tests that test what students can remember (at least for the moment) and few that test students' capacity to use the information they have.

Schools would far better serve children and society by getting rid of numerical and letter grades and finding other means to assess students' progress toward identified standards. The use of clearly defined rubrics is one way to do this. Having teachers evaluate a common assessment given to all students (an essay or science project) using a rubric previously designed by those teachers is a way to help teachers develop a shared sense of what constitutes the kind of performance that meets, exceeds, or fails to meet the standard.

For sure, it will take more time and more training to do this. Certainly it will involve some unlearning, as well as new learning, but the educational benefits will be greater for teachers and students. When you stop to consider it, what really is the qualitative difference between a B+ and an A−, or an 88 and a 90?

If we want students to love learning, we must shift their focus and ours from grades to their learning. It won't be easy, and it won't necessarily be an enjoyable experience—at least at the outset—but if we don't want our students to be twenty-first-century illiterates, we must undertake the task.

In *The End of Education: Redefining the Value of School*, Neil Postman suggested that a teacher begin each term with a statement similar to this one: "Like all other humans I, your teacher, am fallible and prone to making mistakes—making factual errors, drawing unjustifiable conclusions, and perhaps even passing along my opinion as fact. Part of your grade in this class will be determined by your willingness and ability to point out my mistakes—tell me why they are wrong and by what source of authority you question them—and offer a suggestion on how my mistakes might be corrected" (pp. 117–18).

Postman further suggested that the teacher tell students she will occasionally purposely make some mistakes to ensure that students are paying attention to their responsibility. This is one way, he suggested, of helping students develop critical judgment rather than just trusting the experts.

CHAPTER 21

Discovering the Wonder of Science

Carl Sagan, describing his boyhood experience with science in *The Demon-Haunted World*, wrote:

> I wish I could tell you about inspirational teachers in science from my elementary or junior high or high school days. But as I think back on it, there were none. There was rote memorization about the Periodic Table of the Elements, levers and inclined planes, green plant photosynthesis, and the difference between anthracite and bituminous coal. But there was no soaring sense of wonder, no hint of an evolutionary perspective, and nothing about mistaken ideas that everybody had once believed. In high school laboratory classes, there was an answer we were supposed to get. We were marked off if we didn't get it. There was no encouragement to pursue our own interests or hunches or conceptual mistakes. . . . You could find wonderful books on astronomy, say, in the libraries, but not in the classroom. (1996, pp. 3–4)

How many other students' experiences does Sagan's description capture? How many students sit in science classes that inspire no "soaring sense of wonder"—that inspire nothing at all, except an occasional prayer to be able to remember enough dry-as-dust facts to pass a biology or a chemistry test? Too many science classes end up being little more than mansions of certainty where students are fed a servant's meal of processed, pasteurized facts that give them answers to soft questions found at the back of the chapters of their textbook.

Why are students seldom expected to grapple with the kinds of questions practicing scientists grapple with? Why aren't they challenged to conduct lab experiments with unknown outcomes or that haven't been replicated tens of thousands of times in schools across the country? What a shame!

Students should have opportunities to experience the real world of scientists, whose struggles are often as challenging as the labors of Hercules and whose personal odysseys would be, I suspect, as thrilling as the adventures of Odysseus or Ivanhoe. Seldom in science textbooks, or in most science classrooms, are students given the slightest hint of science as an adventure, a quest to find the meaning of human existence. How then can we expect students who have been kept in such a desiccated learning environment to develop a love of science?

Sadder still, in science textbooks there is seldom any sense of scientists as real human beings engaged in heroic, and often high-stakes, struggles to find the means to relieve human misery. Science textbooks leave students with the impression that scientists are a bunch of brilliant nerds easily identified by their white coats and plastic pocket-protectors—individuals who always know what they are looking for and how to find it. Where are the stories that tell about scientists in quest of a certain answer who find an answer quite different from, and even more remarkable than, what they expected?

In presenting science this way, textbooks obscure the real drama of science. Then we wonder why so many students are not emotionally or intellectually engaged with it and just want to take the classes they are required to take and no more.

How many students encounter the periodic table in a classroom or textbook and see no significance in it to anything in their lives? How many wish Russian chemist D. I. Mendeleyev, whose extraordinary efforts formulated the table, hadn't bothered? Yet if students read Carl Sagan's *Cosmos* and discover that that table represents the building blocks of everything in existence, including them, they might then experience a sense of wonder and an admiration for its creator.

What about photosynthesis? It may be a bit more interesting presented as a story with little molecules running around in plants like assembly-line workers using chlorophyll to manufacture food. Instead, textbooks distill all the suspense and excitement out of it and present it merely as a cargo of facts to be memorized and eventually forgotten.

If we want students to love science, instead of handing them mind-numbing textbooks that capture so little of the wonder of science, we should give them books or articles by writers who themselves love science and who capture in compelling prose the drama of it and the enthusiasm of the men and women who work in it

Stephen Jay Gould was a paleontologist and evolutionary biologist described by a *New York Times* book reviewer as a science writer who can work himself into a corkscrew of ideas and improbable allusions paragraph after paragraph and then, uncoiling, hit with such power that his fans know they are experiencing the game of essay writing at its best. (Wilford 1991)

Gould's quirky writing style and eye-catching chapter titles could prove irresistible to high school students. How many of them could turn away from this one in *Bully for Brontosaurus*: "George Canning's Left Buttock and the Origin of the Species"?

There are so many other writers who could give students and teachers a window into the wonders of science: Carl Sagan, Timothy Ferris, Lewis Thomas, Richard Feynman, and others. Feynman, a Nobel Prize–winning physicist, titled one of his books *The Pleasure of Finding Things Out*. That should be the reason students have for studying science—for the pleasure of finding things out.

Lewis Thomas once described science as "high adventure . . . the wildest of all explorations ever undertaken by human beings, the chance to catch a close view of things never seen before, the shrewdest maneuver for discovering how the world works" (1983, p. 154). How many students wouldn't sign on for an adventure like that?

Today, with schools and policymakers so obsessed with testing and accountability measures, students will discover the wonder of science only if their teacher has the courage to steer clear of science textbooks and the current uninspiring science classroom teaching paradigm and chooses to present science as a high adventure through which students, like scientists, discover how the world and human beings in it work.

True, some students might get lucky and discover it on their own, but those who love science shouldn't leave the possibility of such a discovery to the vagaries of chance. Don't we owe it to children to teach science in a way that is more compelling than the way Sagan experienced it in school?

What do teachers need to do to spur students' excitement for a subject that many now appear to have little interest in beyond getting through it? Here are a few suggestions gleaned from those who love science and who love to teach it and/or write about it.

Don't begin with the hard facts and figures about the subject. Begin by discussing what is amazing about it, what is still hidden and unfamiliar. Science still has many dark caverns of mystery, black holes where what is unknown or not yet fully understood overwhelms what we know. Confront students with the mystery of these dark caverns of ambiguity. Present them as challenges to be taken up and solved, knowing that youngsters love challenge and mystery and are likely to respond.

After that, introduce students to the heroes of the science discipline under study, those very real human beings who advanced our knowledge to where it is now with the expectation that someone in the future would advance it further. Don't portray these heroes as geniuses of mythical proportions or as people of supernatural strength or character; they were not, and it is a disservice to students, some of whom might aspire to be scientists themselves, to present them that way.

The heroes of science will suffer little from being presented as real human beings, people like you and me, who had to work hard to unravel the Gordian knots of their personal lives and their work. Students who study about them this way will benefit immensely more from such a presentation. The lives of heroes should inspire young people to strive to be more like those they admire, not conspire to convince them they must merely worship them and their achievements from afar.

Only after a teacher is certain that students have a true sense of wonder about the subject they are going to study should she begin to introduce them to the facts and figures, the grammar, the diagrams and tables they will need to chart a course to new discoveries in that subject. Remember Walt Whitman's experience with the astronomer? Learning is meant to be a voyage of discovery, not a year spent in dry dock in stale, uninspiring study.

Taught well, science becomes an astonishing adventure of wonder-filled intellectual discoveries. That's an adventure students will never tire of and will always love.

CHAPTER 22

Are You a Wonder-Filled Teacher?

No, I don't mean "wonderful." The question I'm asking isn't whether you are a marvelous teacher (although how you answer the question I am asking may go a long way toward determining whether you are a marvelous teacher or not). The question I'm asking is this: Are you filled with wonder? Do you still have the capacity to wonder about the things you are teaching students in your class? Equally important, are your students aware of your capacity to wonder? Do you share it with them in the classroom?

In chapter 9, I talked about bringing awesome back into the classroom and suggested some ways of doing it. One of the most powerful ways of doing it is to bring your own awe with you into the classroom and let your students see it. Just as a love of learning can be passed on as a benign infection from a teacher to his students, so too can wonder. If a teacher has an abundance of wonder and displays it in a classroom, students will catch it too. Perhaps a better way of putting it is that they will not hesitate to show their own wonder.

Now some may argue that wonder—the capacity to be curious about things and to marvel at them—is inherent in human nature, and it is. The truth is that without wonder there would be little that we could call learning. Another reality is that although wonder is our natural birthright, it can be snuffed out (and schools are, unfortunately, guilty of doing a good job of that), not just in students but also in the adults who teach them. Roland Barth, in *Learning by Heart*, captured the depressing influence of schools on adults.

> But the astonishing, disheartening and unmistakable message for school people is this: Life under the roof of the schoolhouse is toxic to adult learning; the longer you reside there, the less learning is likely to occur. (2001, p. 29)

In a utilitarian age like ours, most of what we hear when the subject of school is discussed has to do with preparing students for university and eventual employment, and little else. There is plenty of conversation about standardized test scores and adequate yearly progress and how U.S. students compare with students from other countries. Wonder—whether it is a teacher's or her students'—has little value in school settings that allow themselves to become too focused on developing practical skills for the marketplace. In fact, it is consciously discouraged, as evidenced in this passage from Dickens's *Hard Times*:

> When she was half a dozen years younger, Louisa had been overheard to begin a conversation with her brother one day, by saying "Tom, I wonder"—upon which Mr. Gradgrind [her father], who was the person overhearing, stepped forth into the light, and said, "Louisa, never wonder!"
>
> Herein lay the spring of the mechanical art and mystery of educating the reason without stooping to the cultivation of the sentiments and affections. Never wonder. By means of addition, subtraction, multiplication, and division, settle everything somehow, and never wonder. Bring to me, says M'Choakumchild, yonder baby just able to walk, and I will engage that it shall never wonder. (2004, p. 46)

Mr. Choakumchild is Louisa's and Tom's teacher, and his name describes the effect his teaching approach has on children.

That is why I'm asking you whether you are a wonder-filled teacher, and whether you share your wonder with students. How you answer those questions is important if you expect to bring vitality to your classroom and teach students to love learning.

Teachers more and more are directed by policy to be like Mr. Choakumchild, reducing their instruction to a mechanical art. As a result, the capacity to wonder, which should be so much a part of students' and their teachers' school experience, is being choked out of that experience. Wonder is equated with daydreaming, and in adequate yearly progress–driven schools, we have no time for daydreaming. "Here are the answers you need. Study them, remember them. We are going to test you on them."

Policymakers seem determined to standardize everything from curriculum to teaching practices in an unloving attempt to turn teaching and learning into a mechanical science. A teacher who wants to inspire students to love learning must commit to keeping wonder alive, hers and her students, in an environment that doesn't yet value it.

How important is wonder to the adventure of learning? Many people have testified to its importance. For the sake of brevity, I'll cite just three: an astronaut, a scientist, and a philosopher:

> Mystery creates wonder and wonder is the basis of man's desire to understand. (Neil Armstrong)

He to whom this emotion is a stranger, who can no longer pause to wonder and stand rapt in awe, is as good as dead: his eyes are closed. (Albert Einstein)

Wisdom begins in wonder. (Socrates)

In truth, the very subjects we teach so mechanically in school have their basis in wonder. In *The Dancing Wu Li Masters*, a book devoted to explaining to laymen "the exciting insights that motivate current physics," author Gary Zukov described what physicists do this way:

What physicists do, however, is actually quite simple. They wonder what the universe is really made of, how it works, what we are doing in it, and where it is going, if it is going anyplace at all. (1980, p. 3)

In other words, they do what we should be encouraging students to do more of in schools. To do that, however, we must have teachers who retain their own ability to wonder and who are willing to share what they wonder about with their students.

I was observing a fourth-grade class that was studying geysers, in particular Old Faithful, as part of their science lesson. The students had read that Old Faithful spews out about 8,400 gallons of water every ninety minutes or so.

As the lesson was drawing to a close, a student raised her hand and said, "I wonder what they do with all that water?" This teacher did not reply, "Louisa, never wonder." Instead, she said, "That's a great question; I wonder about that too. How many of you wonder about that?" she said, addressing the class.

When almost every hand went up, she asked, "How many of you would be willing to do some research on that question tonight? I'll do some too, and we can all report back to the class tomorrow." Most of the students volunteered. How many youngsters would pass up an opportunity to research something even their teacher wondered about? I wondered too about what they would discover and what would happen when they returned to class with their information. So I returned the next day to find out.

What they discovered was that the heated water eventually cools once it hits the ground and then begins to seep back into the earth from where it came. Then the whole process begins again. As touching as it was to see that students had satisfied their curiosity about Old Faithful's 8,400 gallons of water, what was even more wonderful was to witness how excited they were to share what they had discovered with their teacher and how excited she was to hear what they had discovered. That was a wonder-filled classroom.

Are you a wonder-filled teacher?

I hope so.

CHAPTER 23

Education for Living

The truly educated man . . . will be truly in touch with the center. He will not be in doubt about his basic convictions, about his view on the meaning and purpose of his life. He may not be able to explain these matters in words, but the conduct of his life will show a certain sureness of touch which stems from this inner clarity.

E. F. Schumacher, from *Small Is Beautiful*, pp. 87–88

Young people, like all of us, have questions about the meaning of life. Why was I born? What is the purpose of life—of my life?

If questions like these go unanswered—or even worse, unacknowledged—life becomes little more than a wasteland through which they are condemned to wander without a map or compass, or even a clear destination. Yet these are the very questions that we seem to have so little time for in our narrowly focused skills-centered curriculums. The result is that even those who choose to stay in school often leave with a feeling of emptiness. They know intuitively that there has to be more to life than just rote learning.

This is where schools are really *failing* students. In refusing to help them address these important life questions, schools leave their students adrift, attempting to find the answers by themselves.

We must provide students with an education that goes beyond knowledge and skills—one that leads to wisdom. "Knowledge without wisdom," says a Japanese proverb, "is a load of books on the back of an ass." British economist E. F. Schumacher, quoted at the beginning of this chapter, poignantly expressed a critical need that any education deserving of the designation "education" must address:

Education cannot help us as long as it accords no place to metaphysics. Whether the subjects taught are subjects of science or humanities, if teaching does not lead to a clarification of metaphysics, that is to say of our fundamental convictions, it cannot educate a man and, consequently, cannot be of real value to society. (1973, p. 86)

Wisdom doesn't demean knowledge and skills; it simply demands that we move forward to something broader and deeper—to, for instance, answering the question of for what purpose we use the knowledge and skills we have gained.

Some have argued that there are no answers to such questions about life. That misconception can be quickly put to rest by pointing out that if there is indeed no *answer* to those questions, there are *answers*. Others who have come before us or who are our contemporaries have found answers to them—answers that are satisfying to the soul.

The answers they have discovered and the methods they've used to discover them can help students in their search for meaning and purpose in life. We must be willing to acknowledge the questions in our classrooms and willing to provide time in classes for students to learn about and discuss the soul-satisfying answers others have found for themselves.

We must teach students that despite the many messages in our society to the contrary, happiness is not to be found in limitless consumerism, unbridled sexual titillation, or endless play with technological tools. Those who expect to find the pathway to happiness in such diversions end up bored, disillusioned, and disappointed. Seeking to fill up the empty space in their lives with such diversions leaves people emptier and even more desperate. So what can we do to teach students to lead more soul-satisfying lives?

TEACH STUDENTS TO REFLECT ON QUESTIONS FROM THEIR MINDS AS WELL AS QUESTIONS FROM THEIR HEARTS

Teaching students to be reflective will not be an easy task. Teaching them to reflect on messages from their heart will be an even greater challenge. As a society, we don't value reflection very much. If we did, we'd be trying to slow life down instead of always trying to speed it up. If we were more reflective, we'd laugh at commercials that advise us to "Just Do It!" But, as John Gardner has pointed out in *Self-Renewal*, many of us have become accomplished fugitives from ourselves, employing an enormous variety of clever devices to keep ourselves busy and to ensure that we never have time to "probe the fearful and wonderful world within" (1995, p. 13).

Yet that "fearful and wonderful world within" still exists and demands that people, young and older, pay attention to the questions it raises.

In *Walden*, Henry David Thoreau wrote about going to the woods to reflect on questions of the heart: "I went to the woods because I wished to live deliberately, to front only the essential facts of life, and see if I could not learn what it had to teach, and not, when I came to die, discover that I have not lived" (http://thoreau.eserver.org/walden00.html). That was in 1854. Today, many children do not have access to any woods or even peaceful parks where they live.

But there are schools. Schools that take seriously their responsibility to help students to reflect upon the heart's questions can serve the function of Thoreau's woods. They can provide time in the various subject areas to have students read about metaphysical issues and give them opportunity to reflect on and discuss what they have read and how it influences their lives. Teachers can encourage this reflection by giving students affective as well as cognitive questions to answer on tests and in homework assignments: *What does this have to do with issues you are dealing with in your own life? How do you feel about this?*

HELP STUDENTS GET IN TOUCH WITH VALUES THAT WILL SERVE THEM WELL

Everyone has values, whether acknowledged or not. Societies too have values and educate their young in alignment with them in a variety of ways. Today, the two most persuasive and powerful teachers of values in most young people's lives are mass media and advertising.

Between the ages of three and eighteen, American youngsters see about five hundred thousand television commercials, making commercials the "single most substantial source of values to which the young are exposed" (Postman 1996, p. 33).

One need not be a genius to figure out what television commercials teach: consumerism, greed, envy, and impatience, to identify just a few things. When you add to that what television (and other media) considers "entertainment"—murder, violence, incest, adultery, bribery, larceny, arrogance, and overindulgence of every kind—it should be clear why schools need to teach students other values that counterbalance these phony ones. The following are a few values that will serve students better.

Caring and Sharing

Schools are places where caring and sharing *are* taught, but we need to teach students to extend the reach of their caring beyond the school walls.

There is so much poverty and need, both in our nation and around the world, that cries out to be addressed. In chapter 12, I wrote about how helping others doesn't just nurture those who are helped but also nourishes the spirit of those who help. I quoted Bill Gates, who gave Harvard graduates a similar message. In that same Harvard speech, Gates also pointed out a reality about caring and sharing that schools can address:

> All of us here in this Yard, at one time or another, have seen human tragedies that broke our hearts, and yet we did nothing—not because we didn't care, but because we didn't know what to do. If we had known how to help, we would have acted. (2007, p. 3)

Schools can teach students not only that they should care and share but how they can do that most effectively. In doing so, they will enrich their students' lives far more than they would by exclusively focusing on teaching knowledge and skills that will only help students accumulate wealth and possessions.

Humility

Pride and arrogance are so much on display and celebrated in our society that they have practically assumed the status of virtue. How many examples of crowing corporate execs, pompous politicians, chest-pounding athletes, or preening movie and music "stars" do we need to drive this point home? We have, as a society, pushed self-assertiveness to the point of narcissism and, in the process, have lost our sense of community and brotherhood. Through literature, through example, through discussion, and through study and reflection, schools can help students understand that humility isn't a virtue for sissies and that it is a better servant of the wise than pride and arrogance.

Prudence

Humility's companion, prudence, leads the wise person to consider the consequences (good and bad) of decisions before he acts. It offers the antithesis of commercial advice like "Just Do It!"

Prudence is an excellent virtue not only for an individual but for a community and a nation as well. A pearl in the necklace of wisdom, it teaches a person to be circumspect and to cultivate discernment. School can teach prudence by helping students examine with their heads and their hearts decisions they have made in their own lives and the consequences of those decisions for themselves and others. In *Small Is Beautiful*, E. F. Schumacher's comment on society's lack of prudence is insightful here:

> At present, there can be little doubt that the whole of mankind is in mortal danger, not because we are short of scientific and technological know-how, but because we tend to use it destructively, without wisdom. (1973, p. 75)

Schools help students learn prudence by teaching them to thoughtfully consider events of history in literature and in contemporary life, not just to objectively analyze the details of those events but also to try to empathize with individuals who were involved in them. Schools can teach students how people learned to recognize their past errors and then worked to recover from them. Finally, schools can teach students strategies for identifying and correcting their own errors in judgment.

Patience

Patience is another virtue too often treated as a vice in our commercial world, which endeavors in so many ways to present instant gratification as an angel of mercy. Yet virtually everyone who has achieved a measure of satisfaction in life has learned that patience and its companion, perseverance, are the real angels of mercy that show the way to achievement and satisfaction.

Teachers teach students patience by modeling it and by having students read biographies of successful people who have practiced it. They have students discuss and write about times when they have successfully practiced patience and perseverance in their lives—and been rewarded by it—and times when they haven't and suffered as a result.

For an education to be deserving of the designation "education," it must help young people find answers to the larger questions of life—the metaphysical ones—about the meaning and purpose of their lives. These are questions that too often students don't ask in class, but we can see the questions in their eyes and hear them in their voices—and feel them in our own hearts because they are our questions too.

CHAPTER 24

We Must Love Children in the Concrete, Not Just in the Abstract

When I think about the plight of so many children in America today, I'm reminded of the story of the construction worker who had a reputation for loving children. One morning, he laid down a fresh concrete sidewalk in front of a new building. He returned that afternoon to find a child's footprints solidified in the sidewalk. He stormed through the neighborhood ringing doorbells and demanding to know whose child had walked through the sidewalk.

"Why are you acting this way?" one parent asked. "People say that you love children."

"I do love them," the worker replied, "but I love them in the abstract, not in the concrete."

The plight of many children in America today should leave us all wondering if we aren't a nation that loves its children in the abstract rather than as concrete human beings deserving of the nation's love, encouragement, and support.

In 2008 there were 15.45 million American children living in poverty. One out of every five children or 20.7 percent live in poverty in the richest country in the world (National Poverty Center 2009). Even that figure doesn't adequately portray the desperate situation of children in the United States. Some who study those figures point out that millions of additional children are living in "low-income families," defined as a family of four earning under $40,000 (Cauthen and Fass 2006), and these figures don't account for what's been happening as a result of the recent financial meltdown and the increasing joblessness in America.

If that isn't disheartening enough, a study by the Organisation for Economic Co-operation and Development (OECD), in 2005, ranked the United States twenty-fifth out of twenty-six developed countries in rates of childhood poverty. Only Mexico ranked lower (Forster and d'Ercole 2005).

One of the most strongly held convictions of the American social philosophy is that education is the doorway through which individuals can pass from poverty to opportunity. That can happen, but if it is to happen, something else must happen—something that isn't happening now.

The political strategy for educational reform since at least the publication of *A Nation at Risk* (1983) is one of blame and punishment. Blame the schools and those who work in them (students and teachers and administrators) for low student performance results. It is an unloving and unlovable strategy, not to mention an ineffective one.

It is a pity that H. L. Mencken is no longer around to point out that "for every problem there is a solution which is simple, clean and wrong" (http://thinkexist.com/quotation/for_every_problem_there_is_a_solution_which _is/11029.html). Blame the students, blame the educators, and punish them all is just that—a simple, clean, and misguided solution that is likely to get us no further than we are now. The real problem of underperforming students is a societal problem.

Research evidence abounds that supports what those who love real children rather than children in the abstract already know and that others would rather not acknowledge. Unless the powerful effects of poverty are addressed in the homes and neighborhoods where most of our underperforming schoolchildren live, schools alone will have limited ability to keep most of these children from forever falling behind (see appendix 1 for articles that support this conclusion).

While there will always be a few individuals who manage to overcome the overwhelming obstacles that attend poverty, they will be few. We can celebrate their success, but we cannot be so foolish as to believe that these few victors provide the template for how a nation that genuinely loves its children should care for those who live in poverty. Love demands much more of us than that.

David Berliner's research in "Our Impoverished View of Educational Reform" proved that poverty is the greatest stumbling block to keeping children from making adequate yearly progress. He also provided convincing evidence in that same article that even "small reductions in family poverty lead to increases in positive school behavior and better academic performance" (2006, p. 1).

Berliner wrote that if we really want to improve the school performance of the nation's children,

> We need to face the fact that our whole society needs to be held as accountable for providing healthy children ready to learn, as our schools are for delivering quality instruction. One-way accountability, where we are always blaming the

schools for the faults that we find, is neither just, nor likely to solve the problems we want to address. (2006, p. 51)

That is not a new assessment of the situation. It is something that we have known for a long time, but it is something policymakers have consistently chosen to ignore, because to acknowledge it means that they and others, not just those who work in schools, must accept responsibility for the problem—and for solving it.

Back in 1961, John Gardner, then chairman of the Rockefeller Brothers Fund Panel of Education, wrote in *Excellence: Can We Be Equal and Excellent Too?*, "In neighborhoods where delinquency and social disintegration are universal conditions . . . the process by which talents are blighted begins long before kindergarten, and survives long afterward." He went on to say:

> We have set education off as a separate category from the main business of life. It is something that happens to young people between the ages of six and twenty-one. It is not something—we seem to believe—that need concern the rest of us in our lives. (p. 141)

This is where educators who love children must assume a greater responsibility. Sometimes love demands we do more than simply care for someone when they are with us. At times our love must pursue them beyond the schoolhouse door. This is such a time.

If Gardner is correct in his conclusion about neighborhoods distinguished by social disintegration (and we know he is), then love compels us to work to improve conditions in those neighborhoods. If Berliner is right in his assessment that even small reductions in family poverty lead to better performance of students in school, then we have a concrete way to show a nation how to improve itself by improving the conditions in which many of its children live.

It is time for educators across this nation (and again, I'm not just talking about those who work inside the schoolhouse) to step up and provide the leadership that our country needs to build the shared sense of national responsibility for improving the lives of all children. If we truly want to leave no child behind, nothing less will be required of our nation than a communal public effort. How can those who love children do this?

Remember that parent who confronted the construction worker by asking how someone who had a reputation for loving children could act as he did? For too long now, educators have remained silent while a nation that is supposed to love its children has been neglecting so many of them. In remaining silent and engaging in business as usual, many who justifiably have a reputation for loving children and wanting to teach them to love learning have become accomplices in what amounts to a national disgrace. That has to change if this nation wants to take seriously its mandate of leaving no child behind.

The national reform strategy of the moment is to challenge states to apply for Race to the Top competitive grants. This is the kind of divisive strategy that policymakers have adopted year after year, pitting one state, one school, one faculty, one student against another. It is a strategy that has failed so many of our children time and time again because it fails to address the real problem of their underachievement in school—the poverty in their homes and in their neighborhoods.

Instead of kowtowing to policies that create competitive races that pit states against one another in competition for essential educational funding, educators must band together and bring together others who have at heart a genuine love of our nation's children. Together those who love children in the *concrete* must fight for the kinds of federal and state programs that will help families struggling with poverty get relief by creating jobs that will provide a genuine living wage. Together they must actively advocate for programs that will help neighborhoods struggling with inadequate housing, neglect, violence, and other forms of social deterioration rebuild themselves.

"Democracy is not what governments do," historian Howard Zinn pointed out on an episode of *Bill Moyers Journal*. "It's what people do" (Moyers 2009). The Tea Party movement, regardless of whether you agree with its policies or practices, has shown us that grassroots movements can be very powerful forces when they are driven by powerful purpose.

Those who love children and work to teach them what an education can do for them should band together and demonstrate for children just how powerful a force for social improvement education can be. When, through word and action, those who teach children are able to rally a nation to demonstrate its love in concrete ways that better the lives of impoverished children, those children will have even more reason to love learning.

CHAPTER 25

Making Education Relevant:
A Micro-Society Approach

The atmosphere at Varnum Brook Middle School, in Pepperell, Massachusetts, is charged with anticipation. One hundred forty-five students and their teachers wait excitedly in the auditorium for the arrival of George Richmond. One senses that Richmond, an educator, and his wife are about to get the kind of reception that adolescents usually reserve for rock stars and sports celebrities.

Two Pepperell House eighth graders, members of the group Richmond has come to celebrate, sit withdrawn in an isolated corner outside the auditorium. They are engrossed in conversation. Their faces betray an anxiety that is not excitement. They are bowed over a ledger, examining it, talking intensely.

What's going on here? Why aren't these kids with the others? What is this . . . some kind of personal statement? You can almost read their principal's mind as he approaches them.

"Holly, Joe, Dr. Richmond is about to speak. Shouldn't you be in the auditorium? Don't you want to hear what he has to say?"

"Yeah, we'll be right there," Holly replies, a tinge of testiness in her voice. "We're looking for the five thousand micros we've lost. [Micros are the currency used by the students in Pepperell House.] We've got to find it in these ledgers before the bank opens this afternoon. We'll be right there, honest."

In the auditorium, students, staff, and press are listening to George Richmond talk about his search for curriculum and instructional experiences that would be relevant and meaningful for kids—a search that led him to the idea of the "Micro-Society," an authentic society created by students, with the guidance of their teachers, and operated by those students. Richmond isn't aware that what's happening outside the auditorium with Holly and Joe is confirmation that he has found what he was looking for.

Why can't students appreciate the importance of what we are teaching them in the classroom? Why don't students see the connections between what we are teaching them and their own well-being, both now and in the future?

How many times have we asked ourselves such questions? The simple answer is that most students just lack perspective and can't yet appreciate what we're giving them, too self-centered and too locked into the moment to understand the value of what they are failing or refusing to learn. Yet, like many simple answers, this one is simplistic rather than satisfying.

Could it be that there just isn't much of a relation between what students are being taught in our classrooms and other significant areas of their lives?

It might seem like heresy to suggest such a thing, but, like Richmond, others have suggested just that. "We know that many students work very hard. But many do not because they do not believe the lessons they are learning are connected to the real world or that the diplomas they are earning will bring them a brighter future," the Secretary's Commission on Achieving Necessary Skills (SCANS Report) stated.

How can we change the perception of students that their education is irrelevant?

A fourth-grade teacher, along with an eighth-grade English teacher and a sixth-grade science teacher at Varnum Brook, took up the challenge of answering that question. Eventually, that led them to propose the creation of a Micro-Society program built around the concept developed by George Richmond in the 1960s.

The program, called Pepperell House (named after the town in which the school resides), would require students to maintain their own working society within the school. It would give them opportunities to solve the kinds of problems they would face later in their adult lives: finding and holding a job, earning a salary, managing their own finances, and a host of other activities that encompass adult living.

Those things students learned in their academic classes (called the Academy) in the morning, they would have to apply to problems encountered in Micro-Society activities in the afternoon. That would give their learning relevancy. The Pepperell House teachers made it clear they were not attempting to "simulate" society but were rather reconstructing the actual experience of it.

FROM DREAM TO DESIGN

The proposal to create Pepperell House was accepted by the school committee in December 1991. In January, the actual work of putting the program together began.

First, the three teachers and their principal had to recruit additional faculty for the program. The additional teachers were selected from volunteers from various grade levels and subject areas, including two special education teach-ers, who recognized the new initiative as an opportunity to get their students into an inclusion program. An inclusion program would be an additional chal-lenge, but the newly formed Pepperell House faculty knew that little would be gained without some risk.

By the end of April, students at each grade level had to be selected. Enroll-ment in Pepperell House would be elective. Surveys of interest indicated there would be more applicants than the program could accommodate in its first year. The teachers designed a lottery to determine which students would be the first members of Pepperell House, as well as the order of those who would be on the waiting list.

Finally, there was curriculum planning to be done. The now-seven-member team met regarding curriculum twice a week from January to June and for three weeks during the summer. By June, working together had transformed them from individualists used to making classroom decisions on their own into a coherent operational team responsible for the success of a multidimensional program.

Some stipulations were placed on the program by the school board and ad-ministration. Pepperell House enrollment would have to be representative of the enrollment in the rest of the school. Since Varnum Brook housed students in grades 4–8, Pepperell House would have to accommodate students in each of these grades. Class size (approximately one teacher to twenty-five students) would have to be the same, and staff would have to work under basically the same conditions as the rest of the Varnum Brook faculty.

Pepperell House teachers had requested four instructional aides to lower the ratio of students to adults to one to fifteen in their Micro-Society activities, but because of budgetary restrictions, the principal found it impossible to meet this request. So to reduce the ratio of students to adults in their afternoon Micro-Society activities, the Pepperell House faculty enlisted parent volunteers, whom they found very willing to help.

Although bound by a restrictive school budget, the superintendent agreed to provide professional development funding for Pepperell House staff to work three weeks during the summer designing the curriculum for the Micro-Society strands: technology, science, publishing, government, and economy. The principal moved the teachers into rooms close to one another, giving them the opportunity to better collaborate as a team.

The Pepperell House designers and their new faculty worked determinedly through the summer, readying the program for its September debut. The af-ternoon Micro-Society curriculum had to be finalized. Every student would have a job in one of the strands, so job specifications had to be designed for each task (bank teller, newspaper editor, judge, internal revenue officer, and others). Marketplace booths awaited construction. Micro currency had to be printed to pay students for the jobs they performed. Hundreds of other details had to be addressed before the program could open.

The team faced the immediate challenge of planning for a constitutional convention that would be held at the beginning of the program. Representative members of the Pepperell House student body, along with the faculty, would determine the rules and procedures that would govern the lives of the citizens of Pepperell House.

Because this would be the first major decision-making activity for students in the Micro-Society, a great deal of time was spent preparing for it. Pepperell House faculty made several trips to a city magnet school fifteen miles away, a school that had its own established Micro-Society program and that had agreed to give the Pepperell team collaborative support.

Throughout the summer, the team worked to put the final touches on their new creation. Through it all, the compromises, the breakthroughs, and the triumphs, team members learned to work together as a united group. September approached, implacably, inevitably. Their vision was about to be realized.

FROM DESIGN TO REALITY: BUT IS IT RELEVANT?

In September 1992, Pepperell House made its debut. Was it a success? Was it relevant?

By the second and third years of the program there was some solid evidence, if not final answers. Enrollment increased and additional classes had to be added. Increased enrollment was an indicator that students and parents recognized there was something special about the program. Comments from students provided further validation. "Working in the bank is very demanding," said ten-year-old Jara. "You have to be careful with all that money. We have to keep track of all the money we take in."

Students don't use words like "relevant," but they express the idea in other ways. Nicolette, a fifth grader working in marketing, said with a determined sigh, "It's hectic trying to meet deadlines. I come home as tired as my mom."

Still, as that old saying warns, actions speak louder than words.

One Pepperell House student created his own postage stamp and another planned to write a book series titled *The Little Old Man*. Other students filmed their own video titled *Life at Varnum Brook* and had it televised by a local cable television station.

Not all the activities of the students in Pepperell House were designed by the teaching staff. In November of its second year, the bank had to recall its currency and convert to a checking account system when it was discovered that some students had set up black-market enterprises and had accumulated up to ten thousand micro-dollars. But that's part of real life too, isn't it?

Holly and Joe never did get to the auditorium to hear George Richmond speak. They met him later when he and his wife stopped by to see the First Pepperell House Bank running smoothly. Richmond congratulated them on their professionalism. Holly and Joe, relaxed now, accepted his praise with pride. He never knew what they'd been through. He would have been even more impressed if he had.

CHAPTER 26

Why We Need the Arts in Education

*Until recently, the abilities that led to success in school, work, and busi-
ness were characteristic of the left hemisphere. They were the sorts of lin-
ear, logical, analytical talents measured by SATs and deployed by CPAs.
. . . But they're no longer sufficient . . . the abilities that matter most are
now closer in spirit to the specialties of the right hemisphere—artistry,
empathy, seeing the big picture, and pursuing the transcendent.*

Daniel Pink

WITHOUT THE BENEFIT OF ART

Charles Darwin described the sterility of a life without the arts: "Up to the
age of thirty, or beyond it," he wrote, "poetry of many kinds . . . gave me
great pleasure, and even as a schoolboy, I took intense delight in Shakespeare,
especially the historical plays. I have also said that formerly pictures gave me
considerable, and music very great delight" (Schumacher 1973, p. 91).

It may seem remarkable to have a great scientist expressing these senti-
ments, but what happened to Darwin later is even more remarkable—and
disheartening. As a consequence of focusing too much on math and science
and ignoring the arts, he lost his ability to enjoy those things that had once
given him such delight. "My mind seems to have become a kind of machine
for grinding general laws out of large collections of facts," he confessed
(Schumacher, p. 91).

Those who believe that an education should focus on practical preparation
for future employment might consider Darwin's loss as no big deal, particularly in view of his accomplishments. Darwin did not agree. "The loss of these
tastes is a loss of happiness, and may possibly be injurious to the intellect, and

more probably to the moral character, by enfeebling the emotional part of our nature" (Schumacher 1973, p. 91).

WHY WE NEED THE ARTS

We live at a time in which there is much rhetoric about schools graduating students who are critical and creative thinkers, who are innovators and problem solvers, who can collaborate and cooperate, who have the capacity to understand and empathize with others—skills and dispositions that the arts teach particularly well. Yet most of the focus on school improvement centers on improving students' performance in math and science, as well as on international comparison tests. There is certainly nothing wrong with wanting to improve in these areas, but in trying to do so, we must be careful not to neglect the arts and the benefits they provide to students.

Writers such as Daniel Pink (*A Whole New Mind: Why Right-Brainers Will Rule the Future*), Thomas Friedman (*The World Is Flat*), and Yong Zhao ("Education in the Flat World: Implications of Globalization on Education") consistently point out that it would be a serious mistake for those who teach students to focus too much attention on logical, analytical subjects like math and science to the exclusion of others like the arts and literature.

In a discussion with Daniel Pink, published in *The School Administrator* (2008), Thomas Friedman said, "It's not that I don't think math and science are important. They still are. But more than ever our secret sauce comes from our ability to integrate art, music and literature with the hard sciences" (p. 2). Friedman was talking about what gives American education a competitive edge in the global marketplace. What he didn't say, because it's obvious and doesn't need repeating, is that the arts are among the subjects students love most in schools.

One of the chief reasons kids tend to love the arts more than other subjects in school is because they get to do something rather than watch someone else (a teacher) do something. When they are in art class, drama class, music class, or even a writing class, they get to be creative, which is what Friedman, Pink, and Zhao say we should be encouraging in children's education.

A second reason kids enjoy the arts is because there is more of an element of play in them than in most other subjects as those other subjects are currently being taught. In fact, artist Julia Cameron has made the point, "Serious art is born from serious play" (2002, p. 112).

Beyond the fact that most kids love the arts and that the arts give American students a competitive edge when it comes to being creative during their school years and later in their workplaces, there is another reason why we need the arts in education. Author and journalist Brenda Ueland rhetorically asked, "Why should we all use our creative power?" and then answered the question: "Because there is nothing that makes people more generous, joyful, lively, bold and compassionate" (Cameron 2002, p. 4).

Well, that's what adults say the arts add to education, but what about kids? What do they say?

Back in 2005, Sophie Mason, a former Hong Kong ballet dancer turned teacher, started a dance class at Saigon South International School. By the third year, 150 students, out of a student body of 350, were enrolled in the program. There were a number of dance performances during the course every school year, and anyone who has seen one of these performances in person or on a DVD can immediately see that Sophie's dancers are self-confident, disciplined, graceful, courageous, and committed to excellence.

If you go backstage or into the dance classroom, you see some other things—a sense of community, teamwork, leadership skills, caring, and purpose, and the mental, spiritual, and physical wholeness that dance has helped her students develop.

Because the creation of art is an emotional experience as well as an intellectual one, Mrs. Mason requires students to keep a journal in which they record their emotions as well as their thoughts and ideas. It is in these journals that we get deeper insights into why the arts are so important in the development of well-rounded individuals.

One student, after confessing that when she started dance classes "my body wouldn't listen to me," went on to say that when she dances, "I leave my troubles behind; [dance] relaxes and refreshes me." Another spoke of being able to concentrate more as a result of dance and of "not being shy" and of enjoying "sharing dance ideas with other classmates." "Dance is an activity to reduce my stress and make my body healthy," another student wrote. "It helps me be disciplined in other areas as well."

Scholars may debate which philosopher first counseled us to "know thyself," but there is no dispute about the wisdom of such counsel. "He who knows others is learned; he who knows himself is wise," said Chinese philosopher Lao Tzu. Citing the power of dance to help one "know thyself," one dancer wrote, "Dance is the most communicative and expressive way to show our inner side. It is like looking at a mirror into your own mind."

In confirmation of the fact that arts increase one's capacity for empathy, one advanced dance class student wrote, "Teaching fifth-grade students in a workshop made me appreciate choreographers' and teachers' ability to be patient with dancers." Another, describing how dance gave meaning and purpose to his senior year, wrote, "What made my senior year valuable was that I learned how to encourage the young students how to create a work together."

It would be hard to miss the tone of love in the voices of these students who speak of the importance of dance not just in their education but in their lives.

If Daniel Pink, Professor Yong Zhao, and Thomas Friedman are right, an education that shortchanges the arts will make us as a nation competitively weaker in a global economy. If Brenda Ueland and Charles Darwin and these dance students are right, an education that fails to nurture our young people's creative instincts will render them less human.

CHAPTER 27

Celebrate What's Right with Teaching and Learning

"Any jackass can kick down a barn, but it takes a good carpenter to build one," former Speaker of the House Sam Rayburn used to tell freshman congressional members (www.brainyquote.com/quotes/authors/s/sam_rayburn.html). He was, of course, referring to the tendency of human beings to focus on what's wrong with something.

Rayburn's comment should serve as a reminder to all who wish to improve schooling and convince students that the time and effort they expend in learning will reward them not just in the future but even now as they are learning. Bashing students and their teachers for their shortcomings is not the way to improve the performance of either, and it certainly won't get us far toward convincing students they should love learning.

Institutions of learning and those who work in them are imperfect. The same can be said of every other institution and every human being. Those who insist on focusing on the imperfections of those who labor to learn and teach make a grave mistake—one that is likely to make matters worse rather than better.

In their article "Leadership Development: The Double-Edged Sword," Phil Ramsey and John McLellan discuss how an emotional environment is affected by what people choose to focus on. In describing what happens when individuals are intent on spotlighting weaknesses, they point out that those individuals often exacerbate the problems. "Unintentionally we generate more of what we are focused on, in this case, problems" (2008, p. 33). Remember the story about the father and his son and the bucket of spikes?

Additionally, Ramsey and McLellan identified another difficulty that occurs when people concentrate too much on imperfections: "Attention to problems, or weaknesses, encourages negative emotions such as anxiety and disappointment, which in turn affects the quality of our thinking" (p. 33). People, whatever their age, may learn to endure disappointment and anxiety, but those feelings don't do much to enhance their love of what they are doing—much less their performance in it.

A few years ago, I witnessed how beginning with a negative focus can undermine the morale of a school staff. We hired a professional facilitator to help us develop a three-year school improvement plan. The facilitator brought together a representative group of parents and faculty in his first meeting and charged the faculty to remain silent as he asked parents what improvements they would like to see in the school.

The faculty sat for an hour and a half as parents described in detail everything they believed was wrong with the school. By the end of that session, teachers and administrators were so angry, dispirited, depressed, and resentful that it was only with the greatest reluctance they returned for the follow-up planning session. For months afterward, the group expended more of its energy on trying to get beyond the bitterness and hurt of that session than on developing a school improvement plan. When you have a dispirited staff, the chances of having spirited, inspiring classrooms that promote love of learning are not enhanced.

Those who want quality learning environments should never ignore the imperfections of those environments; that would be irresponsible. How they choose to approach improving those environments and whether or not they are willing to celebrate what is right with them before setting about attempting further improvement will determine the results they get. If you want to work on an unfinished barn, you'd want a carpenter rather than an army of carpenter ants to do the job, wouldn't you?

The work of both teaching and learning can at times become terribly depleting. That by itself doesn't make it unlovable; human beings, regardless of their age, can endure a lot of hardship if they know their effort is honorable and honored. When it is neither acknowledged nor respected . . . well, there is no need to finish that sentence; we've all been there at one time or another.

It is therefore essential that those who want to ensure quality education and convince children that their education is worthy of their commitment invest time and energy into celebrating what happens in a learning environment instead of disparaging it.

That means that negative messages about school and schooling need to be offset with what both do well. It means celebrating what is positive about them. In other words, if we want to convince students to love learning rather than simply endure it, we need more carpenters and fewer carpenter ants and jackasses.

Here are a few suggestions for you would-be school carpenters.

VIDEOTAPE MAGIC MOMENTS OF ACHIEVEMENT IN THE LEARNING ENVIRONMENT

Celebrate what is working in your learning environment wherever it may be, particularly those things that relate to your teaching mission and values. Don't neglect the headline grabbers (the sports or drama or arts presentations in schools), but go further and capture those magic moments that happen out of sight and out of view of the public eye. Videotape them and celebrate them.

The things you capture on tape don't have to be dynamic; you can make even small successes more compelling by giving your video a background of inspiring music and words.

Make the videos brief and inspirational, and this is very important—carefully time the showing of the video for periods during which those wonderful moments you've captured will have the most impact. Even if the video is only viewed by faculty and students, if it is well done, it will have a powerful effect on both.

Why? Because visual images have a more powerful impact on people than hearing about a success or reading about it. Do you doubt it? Watch the final scene of *Dead Poets Society*, where Mr. Keating departs from his classroom and his job, as his students salute their lost "captain," and see if you're not moved by it. Visual images move us in ways that words alone cannot.

While I'm thinking about it, you don't have to videotape alone. Enlist your students' help in doing it. That's an excellent way to teach them how to look for things and at things—especially things to celebrate. Besides, they'll love doing it.

FIND A MOTIVATIONAL SPEAKER

A school year often begins with the superintendent or the principal delivering a motivational speech to students and staff. There is nothing wrong with that, but wouldn't those in school be even more energized by a motivational talk by a former student or a parent or a community member who could speak passionately about what education has done for him and how he values it?

Bringing in someone to speak during the middle of a year when the enthusiasm of the learning community is leeching away can be even more energizing if you take the time to find that "right someone." Someone who is passionate about learning and can articulate what teachers have contributed to his success and happiness can revitalize both students and staff. Even if a parent is homeschooling, if he can find someone who can speak passionately to his youngster about the value that education has had in her life, it will add some Geritol to the child's learning endeavor.

HELP OVERLY CRITICAL PEOPLE SEE THE GLASS AS HALF FULL INSTEAD OF HALF EMPTY

Not everyone who criticizes a school or a teacher is intent on undermining them. Their actions may in effect be accomplishing that, but that may not be what they intended. The tendency of human beings to focus on what's wrong—to see the glass as half empty rather than half full—is always present. In some, it is greater than in others, and in some cases, the best medicine may be for both the critic and the person being criticized to sit down and have a good heart-to-heart talk.

I remember one parent who used to come to my office regularly with a litany of complaints about our school. Sitting there listening to her was exhausting. One day in the middle of one of her critical diatribes, I said to her, "You know, Mrs. Smith [not her real name], I wonder why you keep your daughter here in our school. If I had the kinds of concerns you continually bring to my office, I'd seriously consider moving my child to another school." I didn't say it sarcastically; I said it sincerely and nonjudgmentally. What followed may seem amazing, but I had seen it happen before in similar circumstances.

Instantly she changed from being a critic to being a carpenter and began relating all the good things the school and the teachers were doing for her daughter and telling me she wasn't trying to tear us down—she was only trying to make us better. You know what? On almost every occasion when I saw her after that, she had something good to say about our school. True, she could usually suggest something to make us better, but her suggestions had a different flavor to them.

By the way, let us not forget that the carpenter ant may be a student or a class of them. This same approach can work wonders with them as well (recall my senior class story).

If we want to make our schooling better—in the sense that it is not only more productive but that it encourages students to love learning (can we really separate the two?)—then the approach we must take to improving schools should be the approach a carpenter takes, not the approach of a jackass.

CHAPTER 28

The Walkabout

I began this book in a school with me addressing an assembly of students, teachers, and parents and revealing to them a seldom publicly acknowledged secret about schooling—that teachers (most of them, at least) love their students and want what is best for them. In the pages that followed, I discussed how the love of teachers for their students and passion for what they teach can result in students not only loving their teacher but loving learning as well.

Yet this love and passion and the effects it can have on children still remain a well-concealed secret to many outside the schoolhouse.

So while again acknowledging that not all teaching and learning take place in school, but in recognition of the fact that much of it does, I think it appropriate to end this book in the schoolhouse describing a strategy that is designed to show a wider audience exactly what love has to do with teaching and learning. The strategy is called the "walkabout." It can be used effectively with parents, community members, and even policymakers. I invite those educators who don't work in schools to think about how they might adapt it for their use.

"Transparency" is the new buzzword in politics and business. Actually, it's a great idea not only for politicians and businessmen but also for those in the field of education. Very few adults who are not directly associated with schools know what goes on in them, and that harms both the students and the professionals who work there. Ignorance is not a blessing in this instance. With that in mind, consider the following strategy for making what happens in schools more transparent to the general public, who should have an interest in the work done in their schools.

THE WALKABOUT

On a selected day, usually one day per semester, invite people into your school to visit your classrooms. Begin the day with people meeting with the principal for a brief orientation that should include what you hope their visit will accomplish and some general guidelines about the visit. For instance, "We hope that in visiting our classrooms, you will get a better understanding of what children and teachers are actually doing in those classrooms and that this knowledge will help enrich your conversations about teaching and learning—first with your children, if you have children in school, and with other adults in our community."

The principal should remind people in these briefings that most faculty members are parents too, who know from personal experience that when a parent asks a son or daughter "Well, what did you do in school today?" the answer is usually "Oh, nothing."

The principal might also mention that in taking time to come to school to see what children are doing in *their* workplace, parents and other community members are sending a powerful message that they value the work of the children and the children's teachers.

Strongly encourage dads to attend these walkabouts as well. You might even provide them with a letter for their employers if they work full-time, explaining why their presence at these walkabouts is so vital.

The guidelines you give visitors in the orientation briefing should include a version of the following: "Please go into classrooms in groups no larger than three so you don't become a distraction to students. Stay no more than ten or fifteen minutes in any one class so you get a sense of that class, but leave yourself time to visit all of your son's or daughter's classes and allow time for other parents to visit the class. Look at the work displayed in the classrooms and corridors and note its quality and variety. If students are receiving direct instruction from a teacher, please do not interrupt. If students are working in groups, we encourage you to ask students three questions: What are you learning? Why are you learning it? How will you use this knowledge in the future?" (I'll share an interesting story about these three questions later in this chapter.) A final guideline to your guests should be a reminder that they are not there to evaluate teachers (that's the principal's job) but to get a sense of children's and their teachers' lives in school.

Once the initial orientation is over and all your visitors' questions have been answered, send them on their walkabout, with the understanding that you will meet again in the same room in an hour and a half, at which time you'll ask *them* to address three questions: What did you see that positively impressed you? What did you see that might have confused you? What did you see that you may not have liked? When the walkabout concludes and the visitors are gathered once again for your after-the-walkabout meeting, encourage them to address those three questions in that order.

On every occasion, when I have held these walkabouts, there have been at least ten positive things our guests have reported for every negative one. Often there were no negative observations, but when there were, it gave me an opportunity to address them with the group, and later with the faculty, if they were accurate.

By far, most of what came out of these debriefings was astonishment and appreciation for what teachers and students were accomplishing in classes. Most visitors were simply not prepared for the changes in schools that had occurred since they had gone to school—changes that focused on getting students to think, question, problem solve, be creative, and apply what they were learning rather than merely sit and take notes. More than a few guests said they wished they had gotten the kind of schooling these children were now receiving.

Now for my true story about the three questions I suggested you encourage parents to ask students.

On one occasion when I introduced the three questions in the briefing before the walkabout, a visitor, who was a school board member, raised her hand and said, "I have no doubt that students will be able to answer the questions: What are you learning and why are you learning it? I expect a school to teach them that. But I'll give you a million dollars if they can tell me how they'll use what they are learning once they leave school."

When the group returned after their walkabout for our debriefing and I asked for comments, she was one of the first to raise her hand. "The check will be in the mail," she simply said. We never did get a check, but the compliment was worth a million.

If you use this strategy, it is important that all faculty recognize that they should not do any special pony-and-cart show for visitors during these walkabouts. You want your guests to see what is happening on an ordinary school day. Nothing will fog up the window of transparency faster than a rigged performance. Rigged performances are easy to spot, and even when they are not, children go home and talk, especially when something unusual happens in school.

Second, take the time to record your guests' reactions and comments and share them with faculty (using discretion if a comment is directed toward a particular faculty member). My debriefings with visitors after these walkabouts produced such a rich vein of accolades about the school, its faculty, and its students that I was tempted to (but never did) videotape one or two of them and play them for faculty and students. If you do choose to videotape, make sure you get your visitors' permission to tape the debriefing.

Finally, if you want students to be able to talk intelligently about what they are learning in school and why and how they will use these things in the future, teachers must talk with students about such things and give them opportunities to see how they can apply what they have learned.

We don't usually hear much about transparency unless there isn't any. Still, in an age when far too many people view schools and those who work in them as through a glass darkly—as a reflection of their own school experiences— throwing the doors of our schools open and letting the light of transparency shine through them may be an idea whose time has come. No one will suffer from discovering what love has to do with this thing called learning.

CHAPTER 29

Never Lose Sight of the Higher Purpose of an Education

"What is the good of drawing up, on paper, rules for social behaviour, if we know that, in fact, our greed, cowardice, ill temper, and self-conceit are going to prevent us from keeping them?" asked C. S. Lewis in *Mere Christianity*. He went on to say that, of course, we must draw up rules for our social and economic behavior, but unless individuals are courageous and unselfish, those rules will amount to mere "moonshine."

Lewis then made an observation that may just go to the heart of the purpose of an education. "You cannot make men good by law," he said, "and without good men you cannot have a good society. That is why we must go on to think of the second thing: of morality inside the individual" (1977, p. 73).

Education comes from the Latin word *educare*, meaning "to lead forth" or "to lead out of." Have you ever wondered what, as an educator or a parent, we are supposed to lead forth from or out of a child? I have. I think it is that goodness, that morality that is inside each of us that is longing to come forth.

Think about it! You cannot make men good by law, and without good men, you cannot have a good society. Has the smack of truth about it, doesn't it? That is why we have encountered so many people in the pages of this book who have testified to the need to give students more, much more, than merely an education in practical skills.

E. F. Schumacher, whom I have quoted elsewhere, said in *Small Is Beautiful*, "Education which fails to clarify our central convictions is mere training and indulgence" (p. 94). I would add, as Schumacher himself argued, that unless those convictions are moral and unselfish, bringing them forth will do more harm than good.

While it is clear that there is a dark side to all of us (as George Lucas has poignantly pointed out in the *Star Wars* movies), there is another side, perhaps hidden a bit more deeply in our heart's core. That is the light side—the moral, unselfish side that resides in all of us. Even Darth Vader, the epitome of evil in the *Star Wars* movies, has a light side, as we discover in *Return of the Jedi*.

One of education's most important tasks, one that all who educate must keep foremost in mind, is that for an education to have any lasting value, it must help young people get in touch with this moral, unselfish side of themselves. It must help them lead it forth so that it can make them good men and women and, in doing so, help them and us to forge a good society. That is why the teaching of values must be at the heart of every educational effort. There is no such thing as a values-neutral education.

There are occasions in discussions about education when one gets the impression that policymakers and even some parents would prefer that those who teach should steer clear of talking about, much less trying to teach, morality. "Just stick to teaching the curriculum," you hear them say, as if there ever was any curriculum that was values neutral.

Even if there were such a curriculum, and even if we could teach a values-neutral curriculum, it would be a mistake to do so. Pause for a moment and imagine what that would mean—a values-neutral education.

Of what value would that be to young people searching for answers to who they are, why they are here, how they should relate to others, and what we are all doing here on this earth in the first place? These are the questions that matter most to us as human beings. Questions about which skills I will need to get into university or enter the job market, while they may be at times the more immediate and urgent ones, are not ultimately the most important ones.

The purpose of an education should never be reduced to serving the needs of what Neil Postman, in *The End of Education*, has christened the "god of Economic Utility" (p. 27). Any endeavor devoted preeminently to that task is best identified as job training rather than education (word choice matters). Nor should education be reduced to preparation for serving the expressed needs of a nation; such an education can result in totalitarianism. Not all nations' goals are moral ones, nor are any one nation's goals always ethical ones. Even the best of nations have their own dark sides.

The purpose of an education, while not ignoring the necessity for job preparation or the priorities of a nation, must nevertheless transcend them. If we are to have good men and women who will fashion a good society, then an education must help students find the goodness within themselves and help them bring it out. Every human being at one time or another—in fact, at many times—is confronted with the same question the Sufi asked: "Oh, dear God, how can you look upon such misery and not do something?"

If that individual has had the benefit of an education that is worthy of the name "education," one that has exemplified the true meaning of *educare* and acted upon it, then she will know enough to pause and listen for an answer. And an answer will come, as it did for the Sufi. Remember? "I did do something; I made you."

What about those who have been denied the benefit of a genuine education? Well, pick up tomorrow's newspaper or turn on the nightly news.

Those who love children and who want to share with them what education can do for them must never lose sight of the higher purpose of the education they provide.

CHAPTER 30

I Wonder

In these pages, I've said that to nurture kids' love of learning, classroom teachers, parents, coaches, mentors, principals, and others need to create conditions that inspire students to wonder. I've mentioned that one of the ways to accomplish that is to keep our own sense of wonder alive and to make it visible to others. It is in that spirit that I share with you some of the things I continue to wonder about as I consider how we can more effectively teach students to love learning rather than endure it.

- I wonder how many teachers these days consider teaching a calling rather than just a profession, or worse, just a job.
- I wonder why silence is considered golden in a classroom and why, in order to say something, a student must always raise his hand to speak. I recently sat in a high school class where this was not a strictly enforced mandate, and the class ran very well, with students voicing many opinions, sometimes very strong opinions. Yet they were able to wait until someone else had finished what she had to say before offering their own thoughts. Would schools be more loving and lovable if students' silence wasn't considered golden?
- Since we are born with two eyes and two ears and only one mouth, I wonder if that isn't an indication that we should do twice as much watching and listening as talking. If that's true, I wonder how much more effective a teacher would be if he structured learning activities so that he could observe and listen to students as they engaged in learning.
- I wonder if our grading and constantly evaluating students doesn't hinder their capacity to love us and, more importantly, their capacity to love what they are learning. I wonder if having to constantly evaluate students has a negative effect on a teacher's ability to love her students.

- I wonder if teachers recognize that there is a difference between education and indoctrination. If they do, I wonder if they recognize where the line that separates the two must be drawn. I wonder the same thing about educational policymakers.
- I wonder why schools spend so much time teaching students what we human beings already know and so little time introducing them to what we don't know. I'm not the only one who wonders about this. In *Late Night Thoughts on Listening to Mahler's Ninth Symphony*, biologist Lewis Thomas suggested a series of courses dealing systematically with what science doesn't yet know. He said scientists might discover in such a subversive approach a method of catching students' attention, delighting their curiosity, and surprising them with discovery that science is "an 'endless' frontier" (p. 155).
- I wonder how many who work in the field of education are aware of just how controlling schooling really is and what effect such tight control has on students' ability to learn and their capacity to love learning.
- I wonder what effect being in such a controlling role has on teachers and their ability to inspire and encourage learning.
- I wonder why we don't see pictures of education's heroes in schools, such as John Dewey, Neil Postman, Francis Parker, Ted Sizer, Howard Gardner, and others. Former Baltimore Colts football player Jim O'Brien rightly observed that Americans have no heroes of substance—only athletes and movie stars. Isn't it time educators changed that by celebrating heroes of substance in their own profession?
- I wonder what those of you who love learning and teaching as I do wonder about. Share your wonders with me by e-mailing me at second career2007@yahoo.com.

Afterword

Learning is the natural birthright of every human being. Whether we acknowledge it or not, we are learning every minute of our waking lives, and some suggest we go on learning even while we are sleeping. It is true, of course, that some of the things we learn might be better left unlearned—such as that it is our civic duty to consume more and more, how to cheat on our taxes, and just how violent human beings can be. The fact that we are human compels us to learn. This is our glory and, at times, our burden.

Not all of our learning takes place in schools (much does not), nor is most of our learning mediated by the kind of teacher I've been talking about in this book—one who loves both children and what she is teaching them. Radio, television, movies, computers, music, Game Boys, and a whole host of other things teach. At their best, they benevolently assist learning; at worst, they are inimical to it, unless one considers lessons in how to be violent, or stories about the sordid behavior of others, or relentless appeals to buy and consume worthwhile learning.

School is, for many, the first place where they encounter organized and focused learning and where they do it primarily in company with others. It is also the place that has inspired many to love learning and to continue to pursue it. Sadly, it is also the place that has convinced far too many that they hate learning (at least formal learning) and to abandon it as soon as they can.

In writing this book, I hope to have initiated a discussion of what I believe will increase the number of the former and reduce the number of the latter. Not every reader will agree with my prescription for addressing a problem that most acknowledge is growing with each passing day—student apathy in our classrooms. That's fine. Our social systems are strengthened by dialogue and debate.

If nothing else, I have introduced into the constant chatter about adequate yearly progress, academic rigor, and accountability an issue that has too long been absent from it—the part that love and passion must play in advancing quality education. I welcome your response.

Appendix 1

SELECTED READINGS

Following is a list of readings that detail why schools alone have limited ability to keep children from falling behind.

Anyon, J. (2005). "What 'Counts' as Educational Policy? Notes toward a New Paradigm." *Harvard Educational Review* 75(1): 65–88.

Berliner, D. C. (2005). "Our Impoverished View of Educational Reform." http://epsl .asu.edu/epru/documents/EPSL-0508-116-EPRU.pdf.

Kozol, J. (1995). *Amazing Grace: The Lives of Children and the Conscience of a Nation.* New York: Crown.

Traub, J. (2000, January 16). "What No School Can Do." http://departments.bloomu .edu/crimjust/pages/articles/no_school.htm.

Appendix 2

SCHOOL MISSION STATEMENT

Mission Statement

SSIS (Saigon South International School, Ho Chi Minh City, Vietnam) is a college preparatory school committed to the intellectual and personal development of each student in preparation for a purposeful life as a global citizen.

Core Values

SSIS Believes In and Promotes:

Academic Excellence

A challenging academic program, based on American standards, that teaches the student how to think, to learn, to problem solve, and to work individually and in teams while acquiring a foundational knowledge base of the world.

Sense of Self

A community atmosphere in which each student can gain a sense of "who she or he is" in the world; to develop self-confidence, strong character, convictions, leadership abilities, grace, courage, the desire to be a life-long learner, and the commitment to achieve excellence in all she or he does.

Dedicated Service

A view that looks beyond oneself to the assets and needs of the surrounding community and the world and finds fulfillment in unlocking potential in the service of humankind. The model SSIS graduate will demonstrate a caring attitude, be environmentally aware, and persevere for the good of the community.

Balance in Life

An academic program that promotes an appreciation for all of life and seeks to balance the sciences with the humanities; academics with the arts; mental wholeness with physical, social, and spiritual wholeness; and future career with family relationships.

Respect for All

A perspective that each individual is a person of worth.

References

American Psychological Association. (1995). *APA's Learner-Centered Psychological Principles.* http://wps.ablongman.com/wps/media/objects/290/297413/APA%20Principles.pdf.

A Nation at Risk (1983). www2.ed.gov/pubs/NatAtRisk/index.html.

Barth, R. S. (2001). *Learning by Heart.* San Francisco: Jossey-Bass.

Berliner, D. C. (2006). "Our Impoverished View of Educational Reform." *Teachers College Record* 108(6).

Brainy Quote. (n.d.). www.brainyquote.com/quotes/authors/s/sam_rayburn.html.

Brainy Quote. (n.d.). www.brainyquote.com/quotes/keywords/pause.html.

Brainy Quote. (n.d.). www.brainyquote.com/quotes/quotes/a/alberteins133826.html.

Brydon, D. (2009). "Principals in the News." *Leadership in Focus: The Journal for Australian School Leaders* 14 (Winter).

Cameron, J. (2002). *The Artist's Way: A Spiritual Path to Higher Creativity.* New York: Tarcher/Putnam.

Cauthen, N., and Fass, S. (2006). "Who are America's Poor Children? The Official Story." New York: National Center for Children in Poverty, Columbia University.

Cavitch, D. (1983). *Life Studies: A Thematic Reader.* New York: St. Martin's.

Challenge 20/20. www.nais.org/global/index.cfm?ItemNumber=147262&sn.ItemNumber=148035 or www.earcosgin.ning.com.

Dickens, C. (2004). *Hard Times.* New York: Bantam Dell.

Feynman, R. P. (1999). *The Pleasure of Finding Things Out: The Best Short Works of Richard P. Feynman.* Cambridge, Mass.: Perseus Books.

Forster, M., and d'Ercole, M. M. (2005). "Income Distribution and Poverty in OECD Countries in the Second Half of the 1990s." http://papers.ssrn.com/sol3/papers.cfm?abstract_id=671783.

Friedman, T. L. (2008). "Tom Friedman on Education in the 'Flat World.'" *The School Administrator* 2(65) (February). www.aasa.org/SchoolAdministratorArticle.aspx?id=5996.

Friedman, T. L. (2005). *The World Is Flat.* New York: Farrar, Straus and Giroux.

Gardner, J. W. (1995). *Self-Renewal: The Individual and the Innovative Society*. New York: W. W. Norton.

Gardner, J. W. (1961). *Excellence: Can We Be Equal and Excellent Too?* New York: Harper & Row.

Gates, B. (2007). Microsoft's Bill Gates: Harvard commencement speech transcript. www.networkworld.com/news/2007/060807-gates-commencement.html.

Glasser, W. (1990). *The Quality School: Managing Students Without Coercion*. New York: HarperCollins.

Goodlad, J. I. (1984). *A Place Called School: Prospects for the Future*. New York: McGraw-Hill.

Gould, S. J. (1991). *Bully for Brontosaurus: Reflections in Natural History*. New York: W. W. Norton.

Hickman, H. H., Jr. (1998). *Rocket Boys*. New York: Dell.

Kohn, A. (1993). *Punished by Rewards: The Trouble with Gold Stars, Incentive Plans, A's, Praise, and Other Bribes*. New York: Houghton Mifflin.

Lewis, C. S. (1987). *The World's Last Night and Other Essays*. New York: Harcourt.

Lewis, C. S. (1977). *Mere Christianity*. New York: Macmillan.

Marshall, J. C. (2008). *Overcoming Student Apathy: Motivating Students for Academic Success*. Lanham, Md.: Rowman & Littlefield Education.

Miller, J. E. (ed.). (1959). *Complete Poetry and Selected Prose by Walt Whitman*. Boston: Houghton Mifflin.

Moyers, B. (December 11, 2009). "Bill Moyers Public Broadcast Interview with Howard Zinn." www.pbs.org/moyers/journal/12112009/watch2.html.

National Poverty Center. (2009). Poverty in the United States: Frequently Asked Questions. University of Michigan Gerald R. Ford School of Public Policy. www.npc.umich.edu/poverty/#5.

Palmer, P. (1998). *The Courage to Teach: Exploring the Inner Landscape of a Teacher's Life*. San Francisco: Jossey-Bass.

Papert, S. (1993). *The Children's Machine: Rethinking School in the Age of the Computer*. New York: Basic Books.

Pink, D. H. (2008). "Revenge of the Right Brain." *Wired* www.wired.com/wired/archive/13.02/brain.html.

Pink, D. H. (2006). *A Whole New Mind: Why Right-Brainers Will Rule the Future*. New York: Penguin.

Postman, N. (1996). *The End of Education: Redefining the Value of School*. New York: Vintage Books.

Ramsey, P., and McLellan, J. (2008). "Leadership Development: Wielding the Double-Edged Sword." *Leadership in Focus* 12 (Summer).

Rilke, R. M. (1986). *Letters to a Young Poet*. New York: Vintage Books.

Rischard, J. F. (2002). *High Noon: Twenty Global Problems, Twenty Years to Solve Them*. New York: Basic Books.

Ryan, B. (2010). "Stop crying foul." *The Boston Globe* (June 18). www.boston.com/sports/basketball/celtics/articles/2010/06/08/stop_crying_foul/.

Sagan, C. (1996). *The Demon-Haunted World: Science as a Candle in the Dark.* New York: Ballantine Books.

Sagan, C. (1980). *Cosmos.* New York: Ballantine Books.

Sarason, S. B. (1996). *Revisiting "The Culture of the School and the Problem of Change."* New York: Teachers College Press.

SCANS Report for America. (2000). *What Is Work Like Today? What Work Requires of Schools.* Washington, D.C.: U.S. Government Printing Office.

Schumacher, E. F. (1973). *Small Is Beautiful: Economics as if People Mattered.* New York: Harper & Row.

Thomas, L. (1983). *Late Night Thoughts on Listening to Mahler's Ninth Symphony.* New York: Penguin.

Thoreau, H. D. (1854). *Walden: An Annotated Edition.* Online at http://thoreau.eserver .org/walden00.html.

Tuchman, B. W. (1981). *Practicing History: Selected Essays.* New York: Ballantine Books.

Vanslyke-Briggs, K. (2010). *The Nurturing Teacher: Managing the Stress of Caring.* Lanham, Md.: Rowman & Littlefield Education.

Webster, M. (1968). *New World Dictionary of the American Language.* Cleveland, Ohio: World Publishing.

White, T. H. (1965). *The Once and Future King.* New York: G. P. Putnam's Sons.

Wilford, J. N. (1991). "The Stan Musial of Essay Writing." *New York Times* (May 12).

Zhao, Y. (2007). "Education in the Flat World: Implications of Globalization on Education." *EDge* 2(4) (March/April).

Zinsser, W. (1988). *Writing to Learn.* New York: Harper & Row.

Zukov, G. (1980). *The Dancing Wu Li Masters: An Overview of the New Physics.* New York: Bantam New Age Books.

About the Author

Mike Connolly has worked as a high school, middle school, and upper elementary school principal in urban, suburban, and rural school districts in the United States and in prestigious international schools in Thailand, Costa Rica, the Netherlands, and Vietnam. Mike is a graduate of the University of Massachusetts at Lowell, with a bachelor's degree in English. He has a master's in American literature from Salem State College, and a master's in school administration from Antioch New England University. Mike's first book, *What They Never Told Me in Principal's School*, was published in 2009.

CPSIA information can be obtained at www.ICGtesting.com
Printed in the USA
BVOW071451150412

287658BV00002B/7/P